A TU BESHVAT SEDER

The Feast of Fruits
from the Tree of Life

Yitzhak Buxbaum

Volume Three
THE JEWISH SPIRIT BOOKLET SERIES

THE JEWISH SPIRIT BOOKLET SERIES
Yitzhak Buxbaum, Editor

THE JEWISH SPIRIT BOOKLET SERIES on Jewish spirituality will answer such questions as: "How can I be a Jew in a meaningful way?" and "How can I be a Jew so that it affects my life deeply?" The booklets will attempt to provide a gateway to a deeper and more fulfilling involvement in Judaism for both beginners and committed Jews by offering elevated ideals and practical help to those seeking to make real spiritual progress.

The booklet format has been chosen so that essential and exciting teachings on Jewish spirituality and mysticism can be made available in an accessible and affordable way to the largest audience. The goal is to further Jewish renewal by reuniting the Jewish people with the rich spiritual treasures of Judaism.

Topics in Jewish spirituality will be treated in a way to interest people Jewishly learned and those well advanced on the spiritual path, but also to interest and be fully accessible to Jews who are non-scholars and to those just beginning their Jewish quest.

JEWISH SPIRIT booklets will try to make Jewish spirituality truly popular. They will be be inspiring, concise, informative, and useful. They will be authored by people of different religious tendencies, who represent a broad spectrum of those working to renew Jewish spirituality.

We welcome submissions for inclusion in the series. Please send manuscripts or proposals to THE JEWISH SPIRIT BOOKLET SERIES (see address on p.94).

Library of Congress Cataloging-in-Publication Data
Buxbaum, Yitzhak
A Tu BeShvat Seder: The Feast of Fruits of the Tree of Life / Yitzhak Buxbaum
ISBN 0-9657112-3-4
LCCN 97-93470

CONTENTS

A NOTE TO THE READER

Although the language in this booklet refers to God as King, Father, He, and Him, God is not corporeal, has no gender, and is not a male. Men and women are made in God's image (Genesis 1:27), and God has both masculine and feminine traits.

The Relation Between *A Tu BeShvat Seder* (Booklet) and *A Person is Like A Tree* (Book)

This booklet, which is for use during a Tu BeShvat Seder, contains material drawn from my Tu BeShvat book *A Person is Like A Tree*, but has a format and some material not found in the book. The book contains a great deal of fascinating additional material not in the booklet.

Dedication

In loving memory of my parents

Anne Richman Weisskoff   חנה לאה בת אברהם חיים

David Louis Weisskoff   דוד לייב בן יהושע

who dedicated themselves to the education of their children, and planted in us the seeds of our heritage, which, we pray, will grow in future generations. — Michael Weisskoff

In loving memory of my father,

Joseph Cloherty, who inspired me with his love and knowledge of plants and trees, and instilled in me an appreciation for the natural beauty of HaShem's world. – Yicara Cloherty Weisskoff

May all my friends who donated toward the publication of this booklet receive a blessing: Michael and Yicara Weisskoff, Alec and Shirley Gelcer, Jane Schuman, Fran DeLott, Min Suskowitz, and Gerald Epstein.

Acknowledgments

I would like to acknowledge the contributions made by others who have worked to develop a modern, accessible Tu BeShvat Seder and have prepared the way for this effort.

PREFACE

The celebration of Tu BeShvat, the New Year of the Trees, is becoming more popular every year. The Tu BeShvat Seder, similar in a variety of ways to the Passover Seder, has qualities that give it a special attraction to our generation: It is based in a mystical perspective, which appeals to people now. It deals with Nature, an aspect of Judaism often missing during the period of our exile from the Land of Israel. Tu BeShvat also fits with our modern ecological concerns. Moreover, since the Seder is not an obligatory observance, its format is relatively flexible. It can therefore be adapted to make the celebration maximally relevant.

I have been conducting a Tu BeShvat Seder annually for many years. It is a beautiful observance– with its delightful display of fruits and nuts, and of red, pink, and white wines. To my mind, it is the "feast of the future." I expect that as time passes its observance will spread to all segments of the Jewish people.

The text for a Tu BeShvat Seder might best be called a *tikkun*, a "fixing" (repair), like the *Tikkun Lail Shavuot*, the Fixing-Recitation for the Night of Shavuot, or *Tikkun Hatzot*, the Midnight Lamentation. Those texts, like the traditional one for the Tu BeShvat Seder, are compilations of scriptural recitations, created by the kabbalists with the goal for each being to make some spiritual "repair" in the cosmos and in the individual soul. On Tu BeShvat, the goal is to repair the Sin of Adam and Eve in eating fruit from the Tree of the Knowledge of Good and Evil. But the kabbalistic perspective of the traditional Tu BeShvat Seder is unfamiliar to most people today and difficult to comprehend. This limits its accessibility. I have tried to adapt the traditional Seder so as to retain its mystic perspective but to make it understandable and accessible. Over the years I have collected a great deal of Hasidic and kabbalistic material for the Seder, and have developed an exciting format with significant group participation.

Rabbi Shlomo Carlebach used to say that one can tell which are the most important holidays: They are the ones that the fewest people observe. Increasing numbers of people are now observing Tu BeShvat, which is a good sign for our generation. I know that the more I have deepened my attention to Tu BeShvat, the more meaningful the holiday has become to me. My hope is that this booklet will contribute to the growth of the observance of the Tu BeShvat Seder, and help others to unfold the beauty and glory of this profound but little-known holiday for themselves.

THE HISTORY OF THE
TU BESHVAT SEDER

A DATE FOR THE AGRICULTURAL CALENDAR

In the time of the ancient rabbis, Tu BeShvat (the 15th day of the Hebrew month of Shvat) was not a holiday but merely a legal date to regulate tithing and other agricultural obligations mentioned in the Torah (such as firstfruits and *orlah*). It is referred to in the *Mishna* as a "Rosh HaShanah," a New Year, for fruit trees, meaning that the new year for tithing fruit begins on that date in the calendar. Tithed fruit brought to the Temple was eaten by the priests, Levites, their households, and the poor. But when the Temple was destroyed, the Jewish people could no longer bring their tithes of fruit to Jerusalem.

THE DEVELOPMENT OF A HOLIDAY

Centuries passed but Tu BeShvat eventually revived. Its origins as a holiday are obscure. But the day provided a focus for our people's attachment to the Land of Israel. It also became a way for us to express our gratitude to the Creator. When we could no longer bring our gifts of fruit to the Temple, we offered God the fruit of our lips. Tu BeShvat became a day for celebrating the trees and their fruits, a day for praising and thanking God for all the fruit-bearing trees of the world.

Another theme emerged in the development of Tu BeShvat as a holiday. The *Mishna's* reference to Tu BeShvat as a "Rosh HaShanah," a new year for trees, was combined with the Rabbis' teaching that even trees would be judged, to produce a tradition that compared Tu BeShvat to our Rosh HaShanah: As people are judged on Rosh HaShanah, so are trees and their future judged on Tu BeShvat. Over time, other themes emerged: Just as Tu BeShvat is a Rosh HaShanah for trees, it is also, in certain ways, a second Rosh HaShanah for people. And because the date represents the beginning of Nature's yearly Spring renewal, Tu BeShvat became a day of spiritual renewal for the Jewish people.

By the late 16th century, the custom had arisen, among the kabbalists living in Tzfat (Safed in Israel), of eating fruits on Tu BeShvat. By the end of the 17th century, the kabbalists had created a complete Tu BeShvat Seder, partially similar to the Passover Seder. The author of a kabbalistic book on the holidays, *Hemdat Yamim* (Choicest of Days), describes a Tu BeShvat feast of thirty fruits and four cups of wine. During the feast, appropriate verses from the Torah, rabbinic literature, and the *Zohar* (Kabbalah) that deal with fruit and trees, were recited. The kabbalists said that at the Tu BeShvat Seder one should make a *tikkun* (fixing) to repair all of one's eating and repair the Sin of Adam and Eve in eating fruit from the Tree of the Knowledge of Good and Evil. Thus, Tu BeShvat hints at the redemption and a return to the Garden of Eden.

Hemdat Yamim describes the kabbalistic Seder, as actually performed:

> At sunset, people gather in the *Beit Midrash* [House of Torah Study] or in the home of one of the community's sages or notables. Candles are lit, the tables are covered with white cloths and decorated with myrtle branches, flowers, and greenery, scented with rose water, and set with pitchers of two kinds of wine– white and red. The white symbolizes the dormancy and barren look of the plant world that came with the weakening of the sun's rays on Tu BeAv [the 15th day of the month of Av]. The red is a sign announcing and symbolizing the flowering and new growth in the plant world, which comes as the sun's strength begins to return on Tu BeShvat [the 15th day of the month of Shvat]. The forces of nature, cold and heat, winter and summer, are as if struggling with each other, one kingdom ending where the other begins, until the red triumphs and the kingdom of Spring descends upon the world.
>
> After reading thirteen biblical passages about the produce of the land, fruits, and plants and studying excerpts from the Talmud (mostly tractate Seeds, *Zeraim*) and the *Zohar*, the head of the

assembly closes with this special prayer: "May it be Your will, O Lord our God and God of our ancestors, that by virtue of eating the fruits of the trees that we shall now eat and over which we shall make blessings ... that You abundantly bestow on the fruit trees Your grace, blessing, and favor. May the angels appointed to rule over the fruit trees be strengthened by Your glorious grace, causing the trees to sprout and grow once again, from the beginning to the end of the year, for good and for blessing, for good life and for peace" etc.

Then the first of the four cups– entirely white wine– is poured. They serve wheat (a prepared dish or cakes), olives, dates, and grapes. One of the company makes the blessing over each fruit for the entire group, and they are careful that the one reciting each blessing not previously taste from another fruit. Before enjoying the fruit, each one reads and reflects on an appropriate section from the Talmud or the *Zohar*. After eating the fruits, they all make a blessing over the wine and they drink with joyful exclamations. Meanwhile, the second of the four cups of wine is mixed and poured, mostly white with a trace of red. They serve figs, pomegranates, etrogs [citrons], and apples. After further readings from the *Zohar* and blessings, as before, they drink the second cup with great spiritual arousal and elevation. The third cup is poured, half white and half red. Walnuts and hazelnuts (or almonds and chestnuts), carobs, and pears are served. The company studies a selection from the Talmud tractate *Berachot*, chapter 7: "How does one bless over fruits? On fruits of the tree, etc." and concludes with the study of *Mishna Kelaim* ... After discussing this selection ... they raise their cups and drink to a good and blessed year for the fruit and produce. Finally, they pour the fourth cup, red with a touch of white, and bring to the table: sorb apples, quinces, cherries, crab apples, pistachios, sour cherries, and loquats. And just as they began with wheat, a grain, so do they finish the banquet with various peas, and drink the fourth cup with singing. Then the pious jump up from the tables and begin to dance.[1]

The *Hemdat Yamim* chapter that contains the Seder was later published as a separate book, *P'ri Aitz Hadar* (Fruit from a Fine Tree).[2]

Some Sephardim, kabbalists, and others today use *P'ri Aitz Hadar* and conduct the Seder as described in *Hemdat Yamim*.

Hasidim celebrate Tu BeShvat with a feast, but there is no set "Seder" (order of recitation or eating). There are recitations from the Torah, Talmud, and *Zohar*. They often eat fish, meat, and other delicacies, drink wine, and conclude the meal with the honored fruits, followed by singing and dancing.[3]

A contemporary Breslov[a] Hasidic leader, Rabbi Eliezer Shlomo Schick of New York, writes in his book of Tu BeShvat teachings:

> Tzaddikim[b], hasidim, and the pious wash their hands for a fixed meal [with bread] on this holy day, Tu BeShvat, which is the 'New Year of the Trees.' They eat of the seven kinds of fruit for which the Land of Israel is praised, which are: wheat, barley, the grapevine, fig, pomegranate, [olives dipped in] olive oil, and honey. They eat wheat bread and barley dishes [*mezonot*], drink wine and eat grapes, figs, pomegranates, olives and olive oil, honey and dates. They add to this all sorts of old [familiar] and also new fruits [not yet tasted that season][4], in order to make a *shehecheyanu* ["Who kept us alive"] blessing, and they eat etrog, apple, walnut, carob, almond, and so on, every kind of fruit there is. And they thank and praise the Holy One, blessed be He, who has acted so lovingly to us, creating all manner of fine fruits to benefit human beings.[5]

Rabbi Schick also writes about the Tu BeShvat celebration:

> The custom is for the whole family to gather together to eat all kinds of available fruits; they [the hasidim] also spend freely to try to obtain fruits that are not common or readily available. They tell all their family members and the children about the wonders of God, blessed be He, how He created each and every fruit, to benefit and give delight to human beings. They teach Torah and tell stories that relate to Tu BeShvat. This is very important in educating the children.

> Hasidim and pious people also gather to be with the tzaddik of the generation [their rebbe], arrange a table with all kinds of common and uncommon fruits, and together sing many praises to the Holy One, blessed be He. The tzaddikim teach Torah about all the verses relating to trees and about the specialness of Tu BeShvat,

---

[a] In this book I refer to Rabbi Nachman of "Bratzlav" (the pronunciation and spelling by which he is popularly known), but the hasidim themselves prefer "Breslov," which I will use for Rabbi Schick.

[b] plural of tzaddik, a holy person

which is the New Year of the Trees. Happy is the person who takes refuge in their shadow and basks in the radiance of the *Shechinah* [Divine Presence] that is on them.[6]

There are thus different customs and practices for celebrating Tu BeShvat. Some make the feast during the night (preferred by the Sephardim), others during the afternoon of the day (preferred by Hasidim). In some communities, the Tu BeShvat Feast is a family affair, like the Passover Seder; in other communities, it is conducted in a communal setting. It is an old custom in Jerusalem on the day of Tu BeShvat for a person to send to his friends, on platters or in special little bags, fine fruit of the Land.[7] It was the custom in some Sephardic communities to arrange performances for the children, who dressed up as fruit trees; each kind of tree would ascend the stage and praise itself.[8] Rabbi Mordechai of Nadvorna had a custom of lighting many candles on special occasions. Once, when he was in the town of Sighet on the night of Tu BeShvat, at midnight, he lit many candles in the *Beit Midrash* in honor of the holiday, even using a ladder to climb up and put candles in every possible space, on every ledge and in every nook.[9]

Siddur Yabetz says about Tu BeShvat: "People eat many fruits and recite songs and praises of God over them, which causes a great *tikkun* in the upper worlds."

A TU BESHVAT SEDER

THE ORDER OF THE SEDER

The Seder begins with recitations about the meaning and symbolism of Tu BeShvat. (Material that is not recited is included for its explanatory value). Afterward, we eat various categories of fruits or nuts and drink four cups of wine. After eating certain categories of fruits, we recite biblical and rabbinic texts and make personal comments. Then we drink a cup of wine, sing, and meditate. (Do not eat or drink items out of order, before indication has been given, or before proper blessings have been made. Controlling our hunger by waiting to eat sanctifies a meal. Before we continue, fill the cups with white wine. After each cup of wine is emptied, fill the cup with the next kind of wine, except for the last cup; bring fine red wine to the table only when needed. Perhaps cover the fruits with a cloth.) An optional practice: Since a holy meal may be made more meditative by silence, a group can decide not to converse for the first part of the Seder, until after the meditation following the first cup of wine. However, do not let this stifle the joy and later active involvement of the participants. Note: Not all groups will want to perform the Seder exactly as outlined. There is leeway for adaptations, and time and circumstances must also be considered. Teachings and tales in the text that are not indicated for recitation, may be recited or told (if someone has prepared for it) and inserted in the Seder. Some optional practices are also indicated in the text. Most recitations said by the whole group are given in English and Hebrew. Recitations are in bold type.

THE SEDER BEGINS

☐ All recite:

Today we celebrate the New Year for Fruit Trees.

הַיּוֹם נָחוֹג רֹאשׁ הַשָּׁנָה לָאִילָנוֹת.

☐ The Leader recites:

You might ask, "Why do fruit trees need a New Year at all?" The Torah commands Jews living in the Land of Israel to contribute firstfruits and tithes from their orchards every year to the Temple. The Rabbis fixed the 15th day of the Hebrew month of Shvat– Tu BeShvat– as the new year for fruit trees, the date to determine to which year fruit belonged. If a tree began to flower (an early step in the fruit-growing process) before Tu BeShvat, its fruit was included in the contribution for the previous year, but if it began to flower after Tu BeShvat, its fruit was counted with the following year's contribution. Why was this date– the 15th of Shvat– chosen? One opinion was that because by this time, in Israel, most of the rainy season has passed and the sap has risen in the trees; this is the beginning of the process in the development of fruits. Another opinion was that a tree that blossomed before Tu BeShvat did so with rainwater from the previous year, before Rosh HaShanah, while a tree that blossomed after Tu BeShvat did so with water that it absorbed after Rosh HaShanah.[10]

Tu BeShvat also represents a seasonal "turning point," when the harshness of winter begins to wane. Freezing winds may blow outside, but, inside the tree, the sap of Spring has begun to flow.

☐ All recite:

When the Holy Temple was destroyed, our people could no longer bring their offerings of fruit to Jerusalem. So now, on Tu BeShvat, we offer the fruit of our lips, in praise to the Creator for all the fruit-bearing trees of the world.[11]

A TABLE BEFORE THE LORD

The Tu BeShvat Seder is a holy meal intended to purify and elevate all our meals, our eating, and our spiritual life. We sanctify the table by giving *tzedaka* (charity), meditating on being in God's presence, reciting blessings for food, studying Torah, and rejoicing in song.

☐ A participant recites:

The altar in the ancient Temple was the "table" in God's House, on which His "house-servants" (the priests) offered His "food" (the sacrifices, etc.). The prophet Ezekiel was shown in a vision the heavenly Temple of the future and its altar. The angel said: "This is the table that is before the Lord" (41:22). Now that the Temple is no longer in existence (and the future Temple does not yet exist), our table must be an altar, a table at which God is present.

☐ All recite:

This is the table that is before the Lord.

זֶה הַשֻּׁלְחָן אֲשֶׁר לִפְנֵי יְיָ.

TZEDAKA

The 15th of Shvat is the New Year for tithes of fruit, some of which were given to the poor. Therefore, it is fitting to remember the poor at a Tu BeShvat Seder.

☐ A participant recites:

The *Zohar* says: "It is written: 'This is the table that is before the Lord.' And it is written: 'You shall eat [the tithe] there [in the Temple] before the Lord your God' (Deuteronomy 14:26). When a person is privileged to eat in the presence of his Lord, he must show his appreciation of this privilege by giving charity to the poor and feeding them, as his Lord in His bounty feeds him."[12]

☐ Pass around a receptacle to collect *tzedaka*.

When giving, say: "'As for me, with charity[13] I shall behold Thy face' (Psalm 17:15). God, open my heart to love my neighbor as myself, especially the poor and needy. And, in the merit of this *tzedaka*, may I see Your face." [14]After the Seder, be sure to distribute the money.

A MEDITATION ON GOD'S PRESENCE

Pious people meditate at the table on being in God's presence. Rabbi Eliyahu de Vidas writes: "He should intend that he is eating from the supernal table that is before the Lord, in the Garden of Eden before the *Shechinah*."[15] The following meditation is based on meditations found in Hasidic books.[16]

☐ Leader:

We will now do a brief meditation. Remember it, since we will do it again later, without guidance. Please, close your eyes. The Leader slowly reads: **Imagine that we are sitting at the supernal table in the Garden of Eden in the presence of the *Shechinah*. We are surrounded by God's oneness. There is nothing but God. All is one. The *Shechinah* is above, below, left, right, in front, behind, within. Think: "I am surrounded by and infused with the light, love, and joy of the Divine Presence." Silently utter a prayer: "God, let me feel Your presence here now."** Pause **Please open your eyes.**

☐ If the fruits and nuts are covered with a cloth, remove it and display them.

FOUR QUESTIONS
A Tale: Renewing the Old

Once, Rabbi Yisrael, the Gerer Rebbe, was at the home of an elderly hasid named Rabbi Avraham Shlomo Breem of Estralank.

"Do you remember that today is a *Yom Tov* [holiday]?" the Rebbe asked him.

"Yes," he said, "it's the 15th of Shvat."

"The holy books say that the 15th of Shvat is a *Yom Tov*," said the Rebbe, "the New Year of the Trees [*Rosh HaShanah* 2], for 'a person is like a tree of the field' [Deuteronomy 20:19]. [Now begins the process that leads to what the Rabbis say: A person who goes out in the Spring and] sees the trees blossoming [recites a blessing[a].] (*Berachot* 43). It's a time," said the Rebbe to his elderly hasid, "when it's possible to renew oneself."[17]

☐ Leader:

At the Passover Seder the youngest recites the Four Questions. At the Tu BeShvat Seder the oldest recites, to teach that, although a Jew ages, he should never grow old. We should always be young in the service of God.

The sight of many fruits on the table may inspire us to wonder and ask questions about Tu BeShvat; wonder and questions are signs of youth.

☐ The oldest recites:

Why is this day different from all other days?
1. **On all other days, we may or may not eat fruits according to our desire. Why, on Tu BeShvat, do we eat many different kinds of fruit?**
2. **On all other days, we drink red or white wine according to our preference. Why, on this day, do we drink four cups of white, pale pink, reddish-pink, and red wine?[18]**
3. **Why, on the 15th of Shvat, do we praise fruit and fruit trees, and pray for them?**
4. **Lastly: Why does the very idea of the Tu BeShvat Seder delight us? What is its mystery?**

---

a. See p.77.

THE SPIRITUAL ASPECT OF FRUIT AND FRUIT TREES

☐ A participant recites:

The Torah's metaphor for heavenly bliss and closeness to God is the Garden of Eden– an orchard of fruit trees. The Kabbalah often refers to the *Shechinah* as "the Holy Apple Orchard." To appreciate Tu BeShvat, one must appreciate the spiritual aspect of fruit and fruit trees. According to the Torah (and to science), fruit is the natural food of man. Fruit is "ready-to-eat," provided by God.

☐ A participant recites:

And God said: "Let the waters below the sky be gathered into one area, that the dry land may appear." And it was so. God called the dry land Earth, and the gathering of water He called Seas. And God saw that it was good. And God said: "Let the earth sprout vegetation: seed-bearing plants of every kind, and trees of every kind bearing fruit with the seed in it." And it was so. The earth brought forth vegetation: seed-bearing plants of every kind, and trees of every kind bearing fruit with the seed in it. And God saw that it was good. And there was evening and there was morning, a third day. ... And God created man in His own image, in the image of God created He him; male and female created He them. And God said to them: "Behold, I have given you every herb yielding seed, which is upon the face of all the earth, and every tree that has fruits with seed– to you it shall be for food ... And there was evening and there was morning, the sixth day. (Genesis 1:9-13,27-31)

☐ A participant recites:

God told Adam and Eve to eat fruits and vegetables. Only after the Flood, did He permit Noah and his descendants to eat meat. There was no meat-eating in the Garden of Eden.[19] When Messianic Days arrive and the conditions of the Garden of Eden are restored, then, as the prophet Isaiah says: "The lion will eat straw like the ox" (11:7). So too will men eat fruits and vegetables, no more taking the life of living creatures for their food. As the prophet continues, God says: "They shall not hurt or destroy in all My holy mountain" (11:9).

The Two Fruit Trees in the Garden of Eden

☐ A participant recites:

In the Garden of Eden there were two trees– the Tree of the Knowledge of Good and Evil and the Tree of Life.

From which tree and which fruit shall we eat?

What do these trees and these fruits represent?

One tree is the Tree of *Life*. The other is the Tree of *Death*. One tree had poisonous fruit that brought death, the other tree had fruit that gave eternal life. One tree is of the *Knowledge* of Good and Evil. The other tree represents *Godly knowledge*, as the Rabbis say: "There is no Tree of Life other than the Torah."[20] The Tree of the Knowledge of Good and Evil represents Human knowledge. The Snake says: "You can create your own good and evil; you can determine your own path in life and in the world." The Tree of Life, of Godly knowledge, the Torah, teaches that there is a superior divine wisdom to guide us through life. Good and evil are set by God. We must use the mind that God has given us. But we must rely primarily on our higher mind, our holy intuition, and seek God's wisdom in the Torah.

The Cosmic Tree of Life

☐ A participant recites:

There is another aspect to the metaphor of the "Tree of Life." The kabbalists asked: Why is it that the teaching that calls Tu BeShvat the New Year of the Trees actually says the "tree" (singular; *ilan*) rather than the plural "trees" (*ilanot*)? They said that this refers to the cosmic Tree of Life. Its roots are in heaven and, through its trunk and branches, divine vitality and life flow downward to recreate, renew, and energize the world at every moment.

□ All recite:

On Tu BeShvat, when the sap begins to flow anew in the trees, our holy intention is to advance and further the life-giving downward flow of divine energy, the "sap[21]" from the Tree of Life.[22]

בְּ ט״ו בִּשְׁבָט כַּאֲשֶׁר הַשְׂרָף מַתְחִיל לַעֲלוֹת מֵחָדָשׁ בָּאִילָנוֹת כַּוָּנָתֵינוּ הַקְּדוֹשָׁה הִיא לְהוֹרִיד הַשֶּׁפַע שֶׁל חִיּוּת אֱלֹהִית, הַשְׂרָף מֵעֵץ הַחַיִּים.

THE *TIKKUN* (REPAIR) OF THE FIRST SIN

□ All recite:

Adam and Eve sinned by eating fruit from the Tree of the Knowledge of Good and Evil. To repair their sin, we today must eat fruit, with pure intentions, from the Tree of Life.[23] They did not control their desire for forbidden food, and disobeyed God. We must spiritualize our eating– and eat with an awareness that our food and life come from God, and with a desire to get close to God. As we receive life from God through the fruit (and juice or wine), we dedicate ourselves to living for God and doing the divine will.

When we eat, so to speak, from God's hand, and enjoy His closeness, we are in the mystical Garden of Eden.

Rabbi Hayyim Vital wrote: "My teacher [the great kabbalist, Rabbi Yitzhak Luria Ashkenazi, the Ari] used to say that one should intend, while eating the fruits [at the Tu BeShvat Seder], to repair the sin of Adam, who sinned by eating fruit from the tree. Although this repair should be our intention all the days of the year, nevertheless, a mitzvah at its special time is precious, and this day is the beginning and New Year for the fruits of the tree."

To eat on Tu BeShvat in holiness, we must wait to eat, until our strong desire for the food is subdued and spiritualized. Part of a holy meal is not giving in, as Adam and Eve did, to our appetite and desire for the food. Another important aspect of holy eating is continuous meditation on Godliness throughout the meal. The "twirling fiery sword" that prevents our return to the Garden of Eden (Genesis 3:24) is the "twirling" inconstant mind that focuses on God off and on, now yes, now no. Only by continuously thinking of God and doing His will can we return to the Garden of Eden.

WHY DO WE EAT MANY FRUITS AND NUTS ON TU BESHVAT?

☐ A participant recites:

It says in the Jerusalem Talmud[24]: "The humble will hear and rejoice" (Psalms 34:3). Rabbi Abbun said: "In the next world a person will be judged for all the fine fruit that he saw but did not eat." Rabbi Eleazar intently fulfilled this teaching. Although he was very poor, he saved up small coins, which he kept in a special pouch, to purchase new fruits as they came into season. And he tried to make a blessing over every kind of fruit at least once a year.[25]

Optional. Leader: Why will a person be judged for every fine fruit that he saw but did not eat? Participants respond. What is the relation of the Psalm verse to the Talmud teaching? Participants respond.

The kabbalists say that God is all-bliss. And He created the world in order to share His bliss and joy with creatures, with human beings. Therefore, the humble, who refrain from indulging themselves and from taking what belongs to others, rejoice when they hear that God wants them to enjoy His world– to eat and to praise Him with blessings. God created the world for us to enjoy. But only when we control our bodily desires in His service can we truly enjoy both material and spiritual things.

P'ri Aitz Hadar explains the Jerusalem Talmud teaching that a person will be judged for the fine fruit he saw but did not eat. To understand the explanation, we must know that reciting a blessing before eating draws down a flow of divine energy through the fruit or other food to restore the soul. A blessing over a fruit also draws down divine energy to the angel of that fruit to cause renewed growth to replace the fruit that was eaten.[26] (According to the Rabbis, each plant has an "angel" that causes it to grow. The Rambam [Maimonides] explains that any agent of God's action, even a natural force or cause, is an "angel.")

P'ri Aitz Hadar says:

> A blessing recited over a fruit that one eats draws down a supernal flow from Above. The angelic minister appointed over that species of fruit is infused with power to again produce more of that fruit. Therefore, someone who eats without a blessing is called a robber, because he consumed a creation that contained spiritual power, and destroyed and removed that power from the world. He should have drawn down renewed blessing from Above to replace what he had consumed. Now, because he failed to recite a blessing, that angel is deprived of that power and has been "robbed." ... These punishments [like those inflicted on a "robber"] are imposed on someone who is displeased when he sees fine fruits and all kinds of delicacies, and shrinks back from eating them. He has "deprived the owner of his goods" [he has deprived the angel over those fruits of his power] and did not recite a blessing over them. The angel over those fruits does not receive the flow of power from Above that would come from his blessing ... Therefore, Rabbi Eleazar saved coins to buy and eat all kinds of new fruit in order to recite many blessings and to effect the good result immediately and not to delay performing the mitzvot. To encourage this flow of divine life-energy from Above, it is fitting on Tu BeShvat to eat many kinds of fruits and to recite blessings over them with this intention. [Although this should be our intention in eating during the whole year:] A mitzvah performed at the best time for it is precious.[27]

A DAY OF JUDGMENT FOR FRUIT TREES

"Rabbi Aha said: 'Even barren trees will be judged.' The Rabbis derived this from the verse– 'A man is [like] a tree of the field' (Deuteronomy 20:19)– Just as a man is judged, so will trees be judged."[28] Rabbi Eliezer

Shlomo Schick of Breslov-New York writes: "Just as a person is judged on the 1st of Tishrei [Rosh HaShanah], so are trees judged on the 15th of Shvat."[29]

"The custom is to eat many fruits on this day, to make blessings over them and to praise them before the Holy One, blessed be He, for through this, the trees will be blessed to abundantly produce fine fruits for the enjoyment and benefit of human beings. And by eating many fruits, a person will be reminded that it is the New Year of the Trees, and he will pray for them [in the heavenly judgment] that they be blessed with fruit."[30]

Rabbi Avraham Yaakov of Sadiger taught on Tu BeShvat: When eating fruit or any other food, we should mainly focus not on its external physicality but on the divine life-energy that keeps the food (as all other objects) in existence. When making a blessing over a fruit, we should cleave to God and intend to channel the divine life-force that descends at that moment, and send out a blessing of renewed divine energy to all creatures and creations– inanimate, plant, animal, and human.[31].

A recited blessing's inner meaning is that a person who masters his desire for food draws down a divine flow of food and other blessings from Above. Adam and Eve did not master their desire for fruit and brought a curse on the earth (to only produce with difficulty). By eating in holiness we bring a blessing to the earth and to all creatures.

Rabbi Kalonymus Kalmish of Cracow writes:

> A tzaddik draws a divine flow from the Source of living waters to all worlds and all the creations and creatures– inanimate, vegetable, animal, and human; all receive a flow of divine life-energy through and because of him. This life-energy also manifests in him and in other human beings as expanded consciousness ... Tu BeShvat is the best time to master one's desire for food. By sanctifying oneself in what is permitted, subduing one's desire, and setting mind over matter, one draws new life-energy to all creations and creatures– inanimate, vegetable, animal, and human. This is evident in the trees, because from this time on they receive new life to flourish and thrive.[32]

A tzaddik eats for the sake of his soul. He spiritualizes his eating. He seeks not to deny himself but to bestow on others; his goal is not asceticism, but Godliness. It is all one whether he eats much or little, as long as his heart is turned to God. Rabbi Shlomo Carlebach said: "If we only had eaten from the Tree of Life, we would not have to eat much. One apple would last us two thousand years."[33]

☐ The Leader holds up a platter or tray with different fruits and says:

These fruits are a sign and a memorial that today is the New Year of the Fruit Trees; today the trees are judged.[34]

הַפֵּירוֹת הָאֵלּוּ זִכָּרוֹן וְאוֹת הֵן שֶׁהַיּוֹם רֹאשׁ הַשָּׁנָה לָאִילָנוֹת. הַיּוֹם הָאִילָנוֹת נִידוֹנִים.

☐ All recite:

Today their decree will be proclaimed in heaven, which tree will be chopped down, and which tree will be planted, which will thrive and which will wither, which will be barren and which will produce abundant fruits.[35]

הַיּוֹם פּוֹסְקִים אֶת גְּזַר דִּינָם בַּשָּׁמַיִם, אֵיזֶה עֵץ יִגָּדַע וְאֵיזֶה יִנָּטַע, אֵיזֶה יְשַׂגְשֵׂג וְאֵיזֶה יִכְמֹשׁ, אֵיזֶה יִהְיֶה עֵץ סְרָק וְאֵיזֶה יִתֵּן פֵּירוֹת לָרוֹב.

☐ Leader: **And everything depends on the blessings and prayers we recite, as it says: "He has given the earth to the children of men"** [Psalms 115:16].[36]

וְהַכֹּל תָּלוּי בְּבִרְכוֹתֵינוּ וּתְפִילוֹתֵנוּ כְּמוֹ שֶׁנֶּאֱמַר וְהָאָרֶץ נָתַן לִבְנֵי אָדָם.

WINE AT THE TU BESHVAT SEDER

Wine ("fruit of the vine") is part of all Jewish feasts and is always consumed at a Tu BeShvat Seder.

☐ Optional. Leader: **What is the spiritual aspect of wine?** Participants respond.

Wine is made by humans who turn grapes into wine. But because we may then forget that nothing can happen without God's will, we recite a special blessing over wine that reminds us that we cannot produce wine without help from the "Creator of the fruit of the vine."[37]

Wine is consumed at Jewish feasts because it produces joy, which symbolizes the joy of the Divine Presence. The Torah says: "Wine gives joy to the hearts of people and to God" (Judges 9:13). The Rabbis asked: "Certainly wine gives joy to human beings, but how does it give joy to God?" They answered: "Wine makes people sing before God, and that is what gives Him joy."[38] [So after drinking each cup of wine, we will sing (a wordless melody or a Tu BeShvat song). All religious singing should be devotional and meditative– to sing before God, to join spiritually with others, and to arouse one's own soul.]

☐ Participants recite one paragraph each:

The *Zohar* says: "'wine that rejoices the heart of man' [Psalms 104:15]– this refers to the wine of Torah. *Yayin*, wine, equals *sod*, secret." [The numerical value of each Hebrew word is 70.][39]

Wine, which is concealed in the grape, is a symbol for the mystic teachings of Torah. The grape is the revealed Torah; wine is the concealed Torah that intoxicates.

Wine represents the secret of the Torah, whose essence is love for God, as it says: "Drink to drunkenness, O lovers!" (Song of Songs 5:1).

Wine represents the secret of the world. The world is like a cup of wine. What person in his right mind concentrates on a cup, even one that displays exquisite workmanship? We yearn for the intoxicating wine within the cup, for God who dwells within the world He created.

Wine symbolizes the secret of the special oneness of the Jewish people and, beyond that, the oneness of all humanity. When grapes are crushed, their skins are broken, to produce the wine of unity. The mystic secret is that we are in different bodies, but share one spiritual essence– the *Shechinah*, which is the Soul of our souls.

Wine represents the secret of our souls. When a person is joyful, he expresses his inner nature, as it says: "When wine goes in, the secret goes out." Wine reveals *our* inner secrets.[40] The soul's secret is its innate love for God and for people.

Rabbi Eliezer Shlomo Schick of Breslov-New York writes:

> One should intend, when drinking the wine [at the Tu BeShvat Feast], to draw down supernal lights and expanded states of consciousness ... Through this one may merit forgiveness of sins ... These states of [blissful] expanded consciousness are [what the Rabbis call] the "wine stored in the grapes since the Six Days of Creation" (*Berachot* 34). Then, a person cleaves to the Life of all life and moves up and down, down and up, through the spiritual worlds. Our holy Sages have said: "Whoever becomes agreeable after drinking wine is like his Creator." He is encompassed within the Infinite One, blessed be He, and wants nothing other than to cleave to the Life of all life, and to be within Him, blessed be He.[41]

MYSTIC JOY ON TU BESHVAT

When we drink wine on Tu BeShvat, our hearts open with joy to the deepest secrets of life and the world.

> The Baal Shem Tov once told a parable to some *misnagdim* (opponents) who criticized what they considered the excessive joy and frequent dancing of his disciples:
>
> "Once, a talented fiddler stood in the street playing in an ecstasy of passion. Many people gathered to listen and were so charmed by his rapturous music that they began to dance, lost to the world. A deaf man happened to pass by and, since he could not hear the ravishing music, was utterly astonished by the bizarre scene before his eyes. Not knowing why the people were dancing, he was certain that they were actually madmen! My disciples," said the Baal Shem Tov, "hear and see the song that emanates from each and every thing that God, blessed be He, has created. If so, how can they keep from dancing?"[42]

A Tale: The Baal Shem Tov About Joy on Tu BeShvat

The kabbalistic Book of Song, *Perek Shira*, explains which specific Torah verses different animal and plant species "sing" praising their Creator.

One Tu BeShvat, the Baal Shem Tov and his close disciples were sitting in Medzibuz eating fruits in honor of the day, drinking "*l'hayyim*," and discussing the importance of joy, *simha*. During this conversation, the Baal Shem Tov said: "Joy is so great, because it can lead a person to an exalted spiritual level so that he sees the *Shechinah*. When a Jew is happy, he shows that he is satisfied with the world that the Holy One, blessed be He, created, and also with all the Children of Israel, the people close to Him. He has no complaints against Heaven or against any other Jew. Everything is good, acceptable, fitting, and sweet; and this kind of joy, which brings a person to have a good eye, so that he looks on the Creator and His creatures lovingly, causes a revelation of the *Shechinah*."

The Baal Shem Tov then went with his hasidim for a sleigh ride in the snow-covered countryside and they took along some wine, honeycake, whiskey, and fruits for Tu BeShvat. As they careened along in the sleigh, the snow was falling and they were so joyful that they felt they were floating on a cloud of light. Remembering that it was Tu BeShvat, they sang songs from the mystic Book of Song that tells how all creatures, even plants, sing Torah verses praising their Creator. They sang: "The fig tree says: 'The one who tends the fig tree shall eat its fruit.' The pomegranate tree says: 'Your cheeks are like the halves of a pomegranate.' The palm tree says: 'A righteous person shall flourish like a palm tree.'"

The road entered the forest, and the horses galloped in pleasure, kicking up snow all over. On both sides of the road an ancient, dense forest stretched out, with trees whose branches leaned out, arching over the road, almost touching in the middle and nearly blocking out the light of the sun. But here and there the sun peeked through the branches, lighting the travelers' path as they sped along in the sleigh. And as they went, they sang another verse from the Book of Song: "'Then shall the trees of the forest sing for joy before the Lord ...!'" Their singing grew stronger and stronger and flocks of birds flying above them began chirping so loudly that it seemed that they were singing along with the joyful travelers in the sleigh.[43]

The Baal Shem Tov and his disciples knew the secret– that God is within the world and always with us. How could they not sing? When we know that secret, we too will sing and will hear the songs of the trees and the birds praising God. May Tu BeShvat bring us to that realization.

GAZING AND THE SPIRITUAL ESSENCE OF FOOD

A Day for Gazing at the Wonders of the Creation and Thanking the Creator

Rabbi Yaakov Neiman taught:

> On Tu BeShvat, it is the custom to eat many kinds of fruits. We should use this time to gaze and meditate on the Creator's wondrous creations, evident in each and every fruit. Because in all the variety of creations, in all the different kinds of fruits and vegetables, one sees the wonders of the Creation and the miracles of God. When another new fruit and new taste enjoyment comes to us, we should use our obligation to offer thanks for the pleasure, to praise and thank the Creator, blessed be He. Through this, we come closer to Him, blessed be He.[44]

A Tale: The Baal Shem Tov and Rabbi Yaakov Koppel

A tale explains the purpose of gazing at food, even before reciting a blessing and eating.

> Once, the Baal Shem Tov visited the home of Rabbi Yaakov Koppel in Kolomaya on the night of Shabbat and watched him dance ecstatically in front of his Shabbat table for an hour. Later, when the Baal Shem asked him, "Why do you sing and dance this way before eating?" Rabbi Yaakov Koppel answered, "Before I partake of the physical food, I first stand in front of the table and absorb the food's spiritual essence. Sometimes I become so enthused that I sing and dance."[45]

☐ The Leader asks participants to stand around or face the central table, then says:

Gaze at the fruits, and meditate on their spiritual aspect: that they have been created and are being kept in existence (like all created things) every minute by God's will. He has created these fruits to nourish us and to provide for us. Why? Because He is our Father and He loves us. After a minute of silent meditation, participants circle the table (if possible) while singing a *niggun* (melody; it is a traditional kabbalistic practice before a holy meal to circle the table to set it aside as sanctified space.[46]). The Leader brings this to a close and asks everyone to sit.

THE FRUITS AND GRAINS OF ISRAEL

☐ A participant recites:

Fear not O land, be glad and rejoice;
For the Lord has done great things.
Be not afraid, beasts of the field;
For the pastures of the wilderness are clothed with grass.
The trees have borne their fruit,
Fig tree and vine have yielded their strength.
O children of Zion, be glad,
Rejoice in the Lord your God.
For he has given you the early rain in His kindness,
Now He makes the rain fall as formerly,
The early rain and the late,
And threshing floors shall be piled with grain,
And vats shall overflow with new wine and oil.
(Joel 2:21-24)

It is a widespread custom on Tu BeShvat to eat especially of the seven species– five fruits and two grains– associated with the Land of Israel.[47]

☐ The Leader recites:

The Torah speaks of seven species of fruits and grains that are the pride of the Land of Israel. The five fruits are grapes, figs, pomegranates, olives, and dates; the two grains are wheat and barley.

☐ All recite:

"For the Lord your God is bringing you into a good land, a land of brooks, fountains, and springs, flowing forth in valleys and hills; a land of wheat, barley, vines, fig trees, and pomegranates; a land of olive oil and date honey ...."   (Deuteronomy 8:7-8).

כִּי יְיָ אֱלֹהֶיךָ מְבִיאֲךָ אֶל אֶרֶץ טוֹבָה אֶרֶץ נַחֲלֵי מָיִם עֲיָנֹת וּתְהֹמוֹת יֹצְאִים בַּבִּקְעָה וּבָהָר ; אֶרֶץ חִטָּה וּשְׂעֹרָה וְגֶפֶן וּתְאֵנָה וְרִמּוֹן אֶרֶץ זֵית שֶׁמֶן וּדְבָשׁ.

The Rabbis fulsomely praised the Land of Israel, often in connection with its fruits. Celebrating Tu BeShvat by eating fruits associated with Israel links us with the Holy Land.

☐ Participants recite one paragraph each:

God promised to bring the Jewish people into a land flowing with milk and honey. The Talmud tells: "Rami ben Ezekiel once visited Bnei Brak and saw goats eating under fig trees. Fig honey oozed from the trees and mixed with milk that oozed from the goats' udders. He remarked, 'This is what is meant: "[a land] flowing with milk and honey.""[48]

Rabbi Abba would kiss the stones of the border city of Akko, saying: "Up to here is the Land of Israel." Rabbi Hiyya bar Gamda would roll in the dust of the Land, as it says: "For Your servants prize her stones and cherish her very dust" (Psalms 102:15).[49]

Rabbi Yohanan said: "The verse '[God gives] spirit to those who walk on it' (Isaiah 42:5) means that whoever walks four steps on the soil of the Land of Israel is assured he will be a son of the World-to-Come."[50]

The Rabbis said: "Whoever lives in the Land of Israel, speaks the holy tongue, eats its fruits in purity, and recites the Sh'ma morning and evening should know that he will be proclaimed as a son of the World-to-Come."[51]

☐ All recite:

Our ancestors treasured the Land of Israel's stones and dirt; how much more did they treasure its trees and fruits. We also cherish the Land; we cherish its trees and its fruits. May we merit to dwell there soon.

אֲבוֹתֵינוּ רָצוּ אֲבָנֶיהָ וְחוֹנְנוּ עֲפָרָהּ שֶׁל אֶרֶץ יִשְׂרָאֵל, עַל אַחַת כַּמָּה וְכַמָּה אָהֲבוּ עֵצֶיהָ וּפֵירוֹתֶיהָ שֶׁל הָאָרֶץ. גַּם אֲנַחְנוּ אוֹהֲבִים הָאָרֶץ עֵצֶיהָ וּפֵירוֹתֶיהָ. יְהִי רָצוֹן שֶׁנִּזְכֶּה לָגוּר שָׁם בְּקָרוֹב.

> On Tu BeShvat, Rabbi Aharon, the Rebbe of Belz, made a feast during which he wore his *kolpik* [holiday hat]. Many fruits were served. Most prominent, at the head of the table, were the seven kinds for which the Land of Israel is praised. After the meat course, the Rebbe distributed fruits to all those gathered at his table. Then he taught Torah praising the Land of Israel. He especially taught about the verses that mention the seven fruits for which the Land of Israel is praised. ... and he ate of all the seven kinds ... for wheat– he ate challah; for barley– beer; for grapes– wine; he ate figs; pomegranates; for olives– salted fish in olive oil; and he ate date honey.[52]

Outside of Israel, there are some who make special efforts on Tu BeShvat to grace their table, and to eat, fruits brought from the Land of Israel.[53]

A PRAYER FOR FRUIT AND FRUIT TREES

☐ All recite:

May it be Your will, O Lord our God and God of our ancestors, that by virtue of our eating the fruits, which we shall eat and make blessings over now, and by our meditating on their mystical and spiritual meanings, the fruit trees be filled with the strength of Your abundant grace, to grow and to flourish from the beginning to the end of the year, for goodness and for blessing, for good life and for peace.[54]

יְהִי רָצוֹן מִלְּפָנֶיךָ יְיָ אֱלֹהֵינוּ וֵאלֹהֵי אֲבוֹתֵינוּ שֶׁבְּכֹחַ סְגוּלַת אֲכִילַת הַפֵּירוֹת שֶׁנֹּאכַל וּנְבָרֵךְ עֲלֵיהֶן עַתָּה, וַאֲשֶׁר נֶהֱגֶה בְּסוֹד שָׁרָשֵׁיהֶן הָעֶלְיוֹנִים, יִתְמַלְּאוּ הָאִילָנוֹת מֵעוֹז שֶׁפַע רְצוֹן הוֹדֶךָ, לָשׁוּב שֵׁנִית לִגְדּוֹל וְלִצְמֹחַ מֵרֵאשִׁית הַשָּׁנָה וְעַד אַחֲרִית הַשָּׁנָה לְטוֹבָה וְלִבְרָכָה.

BLESSINGS

A main spiritual practice of the Tu BeShvat Seder is to recite blessings. The purpose of the blessings of enjoyment and benefit (over food, etc.) is to remember God. The Ari said that a key to attaining the holy spirit is profound intent in reciting blessings of enjoyment.[55]

Blessings as Meditations

☐ The Leader instructs:

A blessing is a short meditation that should be said with focus and devotion. When you say a blessing of enjoyment, your intention should be to thank and praise God for creating the fruit or other food. When you say: "Blessed art Thou, O Lord ..." (*Baruch ata Adonay*), you can imagine that you are surrounded by God's light and that He is right in front of you. Closing your eyes for this part of a blessing helps concentration; open your eyes when mentioning the item of food and gaze at it. A blessing before eating gives recognition that God is the ultimate and also the immediate source of the food. Without His word, which keeps this fruit in existence, it would revert to nothingness in a second; He created this fruit for you to eat. A blessing after eating gives recognition that God is the source of the renewed vitality and strength you felt flowing into you from the food, of the pleasure you experienced when eating it, and of the feeling of satisfaction and well-being afterward. So that everyone present will fully understand the blessings, we will recite them in English as well as Hebrew.

OPTIONAL PRACTICE: AN EATING MEDITATION

The Jewish mystic goal is to be God-conscious at all times. Since God-consciousness entails the most deep-seated spiritual joy, if we are always aware of God's presence, we will be in a state of constant bliss. This level of mystic awareness is called: being in the Garden of Eden. The first Sin, which caused Adam and Eve's expulsion from the Garden, was about eating. So by rectifying our eating at the Tu BeShvat Seder we return on the path to the Garden of Eden. An eating meditation at a holy meal involves a continuous focus on God. Therefore, when we eat or drink at the Tu BeShvat Seder, we should, at least sometimes, do so meditatively, without talking. *The essence of an eating meditation is to be aware that the vitality and the pleasure coming to you through the food are coming directly from God. That consciousness makes you aware of God's immediate presence.*

Rabbi Eliezer Shlomo Schick of Breslov-New York writes:

> The secret of Tu BeShvat, the New Year of the Trees, is that a person then tastes the taste of the Garden of Eden in all the fruits he eats. When a person approaches true self-nullification, totally nullifying all his pride and egotism, he rectifies the Sin of the Tree of the Knowledge of Good and Evil ... He then merits to reach the Tree of Life, of which it is said: "and he will eat and live eternally" [Genesis 3:22], for he is included within the Life of all life, with Him, blessed be He.[56]

The following eating meditation for a Tu BeShvat Seder (or any other meal) is based on Hasidic and kabbalistic sources.[57]

☐ The Leader instructs:

As you eat, notice that you are being strengthened and enlivened by the food. Also notice the pleasure you experience from the food. Occasionally, close your eyes as you chew and swallow, and be aware that the life and the pleasure coming to you through the food are coming directly from God, who has made it a channel to nourish and strengthen you. Perceive the pleasure as being not "from the food," but from the nearness of the Divine Presence "feeding" you. Set your inner gaze on your Father in Heaven, and realize that, at this very moment, He is feeding you, because you are his son or daughter and He loves you. Then, resolve to use this life and energy that you are receiving, to express your love for Him. He is showing His love and giving you pleasure by coming near and enlivening you; return the divine flow by giving Him pleasure by doing His will. Use some of the energy you are receiving from God through the food to serve Him at the table itself by fervent Torah study, singing, reciting blessings, and other spiritual practices. Occasionally, during this meditation (as well as during any "unoccupied" moments during the Seder), it is a good to silently call out to God: "Father" or: "*HaShem*" (literally, the Name) or any other divine name. One can plead: "God, reveal Yourself to me!"

THE FEAST BEGINS

☐ Leader:

After we recite a *kavvanah* (intention), and the blessing for fruit, meditatively and silently eat the five fruits associated with the Land of Israel. Eat them in the order of your preference. If all are equally preferred, eat them in the order: olives, dates, grapes, figs, and pomegranates.[58] If non-bread wheat and barley items are served, adapt the preceding comment, and eat wheat, then barley before the fruits. They require the blessing: Blessed art Thou, O Lord our God, King of the Universe, who creates various kinds of sustenance.

בָּרוּךְ אַתָּה יְיָ, אֱלֹהֵינוּ מֶלֶךְ הָעוֹלָם, בּוֹרֵא מִינֵי מְזוֹנוֹת.

☐ First attach yourself to God. Then, all recite:

When I make this blessing, may I become a channel for renewed divine energy to flow through me and go out to all creatures and creations– inanimate, plant, animal, and human.[59]

כַּאֲשֶׁר אֲנִי מְבָרֵךְ, יְהִי רָצוֹן שֶׁאֶהְיֶה צִנּוֹר לְהַשְׁפִּיעַ חִיּוּת לְכָל הַנִּבְרָאִים- וְאַף לְדוֹמֵם, צוֹמֵחַ, חַי, וּמְדַבֵּר.

Blessed art Thou, O Lord our God, King of the Universe, Creator of the fruit of the tree.

בָּרוּךְ אַתָּה יְיָ, אֱלֹהֵינוּ מֶלֶךְ הָעוֹלָם, בּוֹרֵא פְּרִי הָעֵץ.

Eat the five fruits. Next, we eat a fruit from Israel itself, such as a Jaffa orange. If there are not enough whole fruits for all present, divide the fruits so that each person has a piece to eat. All the Jews present are joined together by sharing in one or a few fruits from the Land of Israel. While eating this fruit it is good to meditate on one's connection to the Holy Land (see p.57).

A FRUIT YOU HAVE NOT TASTED THIS SEASON

The tradition ordains that at a special time of happiness, we make a blessing– a *shehecheyanu*– thanking God for allowing us to reach this season.[60] It also ordains a *shehecheyanu* when we eat any fruit the first time in the season, for God has allowed us to taste this delicious fruit once again.[61] On Tu BeShvat, we thank God for permitting us to celebrate the New Year of the Trees again, and fittingly express our holiday joy by making the blessing over a new fruit of the season. (Preserves made from etrogs used on Sukkot are a traditional Tu BeShvat delicacy. Some have a custom to dip the fruit used for *shehecheyanu* into sweet etrog preserves.)

☐ Each person holds a favorite fruit he has not yet eaten this season. All recite:

Blessed art Thou, O Lord our God, King of the Universe, who hast kept us in life, and sustained us, and enabled us to reach this season.

בָּרוּךְ אַתָּה יְיָ, אֱלֹהֵינוּ מֶלֶךְ הָעוֹלָם, שֶׁהֶחֱיָינוּ וְקִיְּמָנוּ וְהִגִּיעָנוּ לַזְּמַן הַזֶּה.

☐ Eat the fruit.

A Tale: The Fruits of the Righteous Are Their Deeds

When Rabbi Yitzhak Isaac, the Rebbe of Spinka, sat at his Tu BeShvat Feast, he had on his table, for the blessing of *shehecheyanu*, the seven kinds of fruits and grains for which the Land of Israel is praised, together with fruit preserves made from an etrog that had been used for the mitzvah of the four species on Sukkot[62]. When the hasidim pressed toward the table to receive fruit from the Rebbe for the blessing, he joked: "There are fruits enough for everyone; there's no need to push! Which fruits? It says in the *Mishna*[63]: 'These are the deeds whose *fruits* [rewards] a person eats in this world [as "interest"], while the "principal" remains for him in the World-to-Come ...'."[64]

Which deeds are rewarded even in this world? [The *Mishna* continues:] "honoring father and mother; doing deeds of kindness; early attendance at the *Beit Midrash* morning and evening; hospitality; visiting the sick; outfitting a poor bride; attending the dead to the grave; and making peace between people. But the study of Torah is equal to them all."[65]

A Tale: The Baal Shem Tov and the Orchard in Winter

Once, during the winter, the Baal Shem Tov was traveling in Russia with a disciple named Rabbi Moshe Shoham. They were traveling through the snow-covered countryside in a horse-drawn sleigh. One day, they realized that it was the 15th of Shvat, and they had no fruit to celebrate the holiday. So the Baal Shem Tov said to drive the sleigh off the main road and into the fields. After going a short distance they came upon a field that was not only free of snow, but had in it an orange orchard; It was not even cold there; the climate was tropical! They immediately went over, picked some oranges, and joyfully made the blessings, over fruit and *shehecheyanu*, to celebrate the holiday. Rabbi Moshe Shoham also took a few oranges back to the sleigh, to eat later. All this time, he did not even wonder: How does an orange orchard, with a tropical climate, suddenly appear in the Russian countryside in the middle of winter? Being often around the Baal Shem Tov he was so used to miracles that such events did not even cause him to marvel!

As they continued their journey, Rabbi Moshe regretted that he had not taken even more oranges. When they got back to the main road, for one reason or another, the Baal Shem Tov decided to rest briefly, and Rabbi Moshe took the opportunity to return to the orchard. He followed the path of the sleigh tracks to that field, but when he reached it, there was no orchard! And when he returned to the sleigh, the few oranges that he had picked and put in the sleigh had also disappeared. When he asked the Baal Shem Tov about this, the Baal Shem told him, "When I felt unhappy about having no fruit and not being able to celebrate Tu BeShvat, I brought [by mystical means] an orchard from the Land of Israel here. But since the purpose was to perform a mitzvah, not for personal benefit, the orchard and the few fruit you had taken disappeared afterward."[66]

Tu BeShvat brings the Land of Israel to Jews in the diaspora. This tale also teaches that, in eating on Tu BeShvat, we should not let our appetite control us. Although we should enjoy the fruits, our goal should not be physical pleasure, but the joy and bliss of God's nearness when we do His will.

THE FEAST OF FRUITS IN THE COMING WORLD

☐ A participant recites:

The *Midrash* says: "A feast is prepared for the righteous in the Garden of Eden. The Holy One, blessed be He, so to speak, will sit at the head of the table and all the righteous will sit at His feet. He will have them served all kinds of fruit from the Garden and will feed them from the Tree of Life."[67]

At the future feast, the Holy One, blessed be He, will say: "My children, you satisfied Me with the fruits of your mitzvot and good deeds. Now let Me satisfy you with fruits, and feed you the reward of your deeds."

A NEW YEAR FOR TREES AND PEOPLE

Tu BeShvat is the New Year, the Rosh HaShanah, of the Fruit Trees. It is also a New Year for the Jewish people, a time for repentance and renewal, for renewing the life-force and starting over again.

☐ All recite:

Today is the Rosh HaShanah, the New Year, of the Trees. It is also a Rosh HaShanah for us, for "a person is like a tree of the field" [Deuteronomy 20:19][68] **Now, when the trees begin to renew themselves and prepare to produce new fruits, each of us should consider how to renew himself to produce new fruits in the service of God.**

הַיּוֹם רֹאשׁ הַשָּׁנָה לָאִילָנוֹת וְגַם לָנוּ, כִּי הָאָדָם עֵץ הַשָּׂדֶה. כָּעֵת כַּאֲשֶׁר הָאִילָנוֹת מִתְחַדְּשִׁים וּמְכוֹנְנִים לִתֵּן פֵּירוֹת מֶחָדָשׁ, כָּל אָדָם חַיָּב לַחֲשֹׁב אֵיךְ לְחַדֵּשׁ אֶת עַצְמוֹ לִתֵּן פֵּירוֹת מֶחָדָשׁ בַּעֲבוֹדַת יְיָ.

HIDDUSHIM– "NEW FRUIT" OF TORAH INSIGHTS

☐ A participant recites:

Happy is the person
Who has not walked in the counsel of the wicked,
Nor stood in the way of sinners,
Nor sat in the seat of the scornful.
But his delight is in the Torah of the Lord;
And in His Torah does he meditate day and night.
He shall be like a tree planted by streams of water,
That brings forth its fruit in its season,
And whose leaf does not wither;
And in whatsoever he does he shall prosper. (Psalm 1)

☐ A participant recites:

Every Jew is given his own unique "portion" in the Torah. He has
a special ability to develop new insights (*hiddushim*) in that portion
and to reveal its hidden secrets. On Tu BeShvat, when we celebrate
the renewal of the divine flow of life-energy from the cosmic Tree of
Life, the power to develop new Torah insights is also renewed.[69] Tu
BeShvat is the New Year for the fruit trees and also the New Year
for the "fruits" of the tree of the Torah.

☐ All recite:

May our relation to the Torah be renewed today. May our eyes be
opened to see wonders in Your Torah.

יְהִי רָצוֹן שֶׁ יִתְחַדֵּשׁ קִשְׁרֵינוּ אֶל הַתּוֹרָה הַקְּדוֹשָׁה. גַּל עֵינֵינוּ וְנַבִּיטָה
נִפְלָאוֹת מִתּוֹרָתֶיךָ.

☐ Participants recite one section each:

Jeremiah describes how God called him to be a prophet:

> Then the Lord put forth His hand and touched my mouth;
> and the Lord said to me, "Behold, I have put My words in
> your mouth. See, I have set you this day over nations and over
> kingdoms, to pluck up and to break down, to destroy and to
> overthrow, to build and to plant." And the word of the Lord
> came to me, saying, "Jeremiah, what do you see?" And I said,
> "I see an almond [*shaked*] rod." Then the Lord said to me,
> "You have seen well, for I will hasten [*shoked*] to bring My
> word to pass." (1:11-12)

Jeremiah gazed on the almond rod and received a divine message.
By gazing at a fruit or nut on Tu BeShvat, we too, if we are worthy,
may receive a divine message.

The Kabbalah teaches:

> Rabbi Akiba said: "Everything that the Holy One has made
> can teach us profound lessons, as it says: 'The Lord has made
> all things [to teach us wisdom] concerning Himself'" (Proverbs
> 16:4). ... Rabbi Yehudah said: "That which God has made on
> earth corresponds to that which He made in heaven, and all
> things below are symbols of that which is Above." (*Zohar*,
> Exodus 15b-16a)

Rabbi Yissachar Dov Ber, the Rebbe of Wolborz, said:
> The Holy One, blessed be He, created everything in this world so that a person can learn from it a way to refine his character and perfect his soul .... For, aside from the Torah that He gave us ... He created the world so that a person can learn wisdom from every created thing, as it says in Job (35): "Who teaches us from the beasts of the earth and instructs us from the birds of the air." [Another verse says:] "A person is [like] a tree of the field." [So we can learn from the trees also, and from fruits.][70]

A Tale: Meditation on an Apple

Rabbi Yaakov of Melitz had a custom every *Erev Shabbat*, to cut an apple in two, then to sit down and meditate on it. When an apple is cut in two there can be seen inside ten points [vascular bundles arranged in a circle between the pith and the cortex of the apple]. Rabbi Yaakov meditated on the hint in these ten points, for the Rabbis teach that God keeps the world, which He created with Ten Sayings ["Let there be light!," etc.], in existence because of the tzaddikim who obey the Ten Commandments that contain the whole Torah. Rabbi Yaakov later distributed pieces of this apple to his hasidim at the Friday night Shabbat meal.[71]

A Tale: Eating a Leaf

Once I [Yitzhak Buxbaum] was walking with Rabbi Shlomo Carlebach on Shabbat, and his little daughter picked up a leaf to carry it (carrying outside on the street is forbidden on Shabbat). Shlomo *pleaded* with her to put it down; he did not *tell* her to do it. That was Shlomo's way: never to command or order. Shlomo told me then that his daughter once gave him a leaf and said, "Daddy, eat this leaf!" Shlomo said that he ate it. "Because," he said: "all her life there'll be millions of people who'll tell her: 'If it occurred to you, it's stupid!'" He wanted her to know that if some thought fell into her brain, her father took it seriously. If it occurred to her that he should eat a leaf, *there's something to it*. The spiritual level of following the first thought that falls into one's brain is the level of Elijah the prophet, of the holy spirit, of divine inspiration.

Personal Reflections and Comments

☐ Leader:

At this table before God, at this holy feast, if we gaze at a fruit and turn our mind and heart to God, He may send us insights of divine wisdom and spiritual lessons from fruits and fruit trees. Everyone should feel free to share whatever thoughts occur to him– to tell a personal story, express a thought, ask a question– even if it seems to have nothing to do with Tu BeShvat or with religion.

☐ All recite:

If a person directs his mind and heart to God, in purity and holiness, God will send him pure and holy thoughts.

☐ Leader:

Gaze at any of the fruits before you on the table. What thoughts come to mind? Participants comment.

FOUR WORLDS AND CATEGORIES OF FRUITS

☐ The Leader reads the following aloud or explains in his own words the kabbalistic scheme of the four worlds and its connection to the categories of fruits:

The Kabbalah speaks of four worlds. Each lower world is farther from the Infinite One and a more contracted manifestation of divine reality; it receives its life and vitality from the world above it. Each higher world is within the world below it as its essence, and each lower world is a garment for the world above it. In order, from above to below, the worlds are: *Atzilut* (Nearness [to God] or Emanation [from God]), *Beriah* (Creation), *Yetzirah* (Formation), and *Asiyah* (Action; this is our world). The mystic goal is to reach God at the center of reality.

In the Tu BeShvat Seder, fruits and nuts are considered to fall into categories that represent three of the four worlds. The connection between fruits and worlds is based on the fact that the word used in Kabbalah for a negative force that conceals Godliness is *kelippa*, Shell (by extension, the term can also mean "pit"). *Asiyah* is represented by fruits and nuts with an inedible outer shell and an edible inside, because in this world the path to the center is blocked at the start. *Yetzirah* is represented by fruits with a soft, edible outside but a hard inner pit, because in this world one is closer to God but the center is still blocked. *Beriah* is represented by fruits that are totally soft and edible (seeds are considered edible), because this world is nearer to God and there is no obstacle to communion with Him. Although *Atzilut* cannot be symbolized by a fruit's physical characteristics, it can be suggested by a fragrant fruit's scent.

Rabbi Moshe Hagiz wrote: "To draw a divine flow to the soul from the world of *Atzilut*, one must make a blessing over, and inhale, the fragrance of an etrog."[72] The Rabbis say that a pleasant scent delights and benefits the soul but not the body. They also teach: "Someone who smells an etrog or a quince, blesses: 'Blessed art Thou, O Lord our God, King of the Universe, who gives a good fragrance to fruits.'"[73] At a TuBeShvat Seder, one may smell a fragrant fruit and recite this blessing.

Optional Practice: Getting Close to God: Exercises in Developing Resolve

To make these kabbalistic concepts personally relevant, the following exercises may be done in connection with each category of fruit at a Tu BeShvat Seder.

Fruit with a Shell: Hold a walnut or other unshelled nut in your hand. Look at it. You would like to eat the delicious nut inside but the shell prevents you. Close your eyes and ask yourself: What ego-shell, what self-created barriers, separate me from God? After considering what they are, resolve to break through those barriers. Open your eyes. Take a nutcracker, crack open the nut, and, as you eat it with eyes closed, think: If I try, I'll succeed and get close to God. [If nutcrackers cannot be arranged for a group, do the exercise with pistachios or other unshelled nuts that can be opened by hand.]

Fruit with a Pit: Take a peach or other stone fruit in your hand. Look at it. Eat the fruit. Look at the messy pit you are left with in your hand. Close your eyes and ask yourself: What inner resentments or regrets am I carrying around within me, that keep me from God? Resolve to free yourself from them. Throw the pit into the garbage. Think: I will rid myself of those hindrances that keep me from God.

Fruit without a Shell, Rind, or Pit: Take a totally edible fruit, like seedless grapes. Look at them. Eat them with eyes closed and think: How delicious they are! Then ask yourself: Where in my life do I feel at one with God? How can I become closer to Him in more aspects of my life? Surely, closeness to God will bring me joy beyond any worldly pleasures.[74]

Fragrant Fruit: Inhale the scent of a fragrant fruit. Think: What hints of higher spiritual levels can I detect in my life? What can I aspire to?

If these exercises are performed with a group, after each exercise, lasting a minute or two, the Leader can ask participants to share their thoughts.

Optional Practice: Interpersonal Relationships: Discussion

The soul yearns to cleave to God; it also yearns to cleave to all other souls. Closeness to people and to God are intimately related.

☐ Leader:

The three categories of fruits may symbolize different ways of relating to other people. Sometimes, one is guarded with another person. One puts up an outer shell, like the shell of the fruits of *Asiyah*. At other times, one is more open, but still conceals one's inner self within a protective shell, like the pit of the fruits of *Yetzirah*. Sometimes, however, one reveals one's inner self and shares deeply with another person; then, there is no inner or outer shell, like the totally soft fruits of *Beriah*.[75]

The more a person trusts God, the more he will be able to trust people and be open with them. Does anyone have any thoughts, insights, or stories to share about experiences relating to these different ways with people? How can we increase our trust and openness to people? Or when is it good to be guarded?

THE FOUR CUPS OF WINE

Four cups of wine are consumed at a Tu BeShvat Seder– white, pale pink (white with a touch of red), reddish-pink (red with a touch of white), and red.[76]

The Wine Stored in the Grapes

The four cups of wine at the Passover Seder recall the four times the Jewish people's redemption from Egypt is mentioned in the Torah.

The Tu BeShvat Seder prefigures the feast that God will make for the righteous in the Garden of Eden, when He will serve them fruits from the Tree of Life[77] and "wine stored in the grapes since the Six Days of Creation." The legendary wine symbolizes intoxicating joy. The feast symbolizes the spiritual reward that God has prepared for the righteous, since the beginning of Creation. The "river" that waters Eden (which means "delight") is equivalent to the "wine stored in the grapes." That River of Wine is the ever-flowing delight that comes from closeness to God.

☐ A participant recites:

"A river went out from Eden to water the Garden" (Genesis 2:10)– This is the wine stored in the grapes since the Six Days of Creation. "And it divided into four principal rivers" (ibid.)– These are the four cups of wine we drink at the Tu BeShvat Seder.[78]

‟וְנָהָר יֹצֵא מֵעֵדֶן לְהַשְׁקוֹת אֶת הַגָּן"- זֶה יַיִן הַמְשֻׁמָּר בַּעֲנָבָיו מִשֵּׁשֶׁת יְמֵי בְּרֵאשִׁית. "וּמִשָּׁם יִפָּרֵד וְהָיָה לְאַרְבָּעָה רָאשִׁים"- אֵלּוּ אַרְבָּעָה כּוֹסוֹת יַיִן שֶׁל סֵדֶר ט״ו בִּשְׁבָט.

☐ The Leader explains:

The four cups of wine signify the four worlds: *Atzilut, Beriah, Yetzirah,* and *Asiyah.* As we drink each successive cup, we draw down Godliness from Above, further and further, until we bring it into this world. And with each cup, we ascend to a higher world. In human terms, the four worlds are associated: *Asiyah,* with the body

44

and action; *Yetzirah*, with feelings, speech, and song; *Beriah* with thought; and *Atzilut* with beyond thought.

☐ The Leader recites:

At the Passover Seder we celebrate the past redemption of the Jewish people from Egypt and anticipate our future redemption and return to the land of Israel.

☐ All recite:

At the Tu BeShvat Seder we look forward to the redemption of all humanity and our return to the Garden of Eden.

בְּסֵדֶר ט"וּ בִּשְׁבָט אֲנַחְנוּ מְצַפִּים לִגְאֻלַּת כָּל הָאֱנוֹשׁוּת כֻּלּוֹ וְשִׁבְתֵינוּ לְגַן עֵדֶן.

The Colors of the Four Cups of Wine

We drink four cups of wine: white, pale pink, reddish-pink, then red. The gradual change in color symbolizes the seasonal change in the colors of Nature as the growing year progresses, from the stark, cold white of winter, to the beginnings of springtime warmth, and into the vital, vibrant shades of summer.[79] God established the seasons necessary for fruit trees and other crops, and, after the Flood, He promised Noah that they would never again be changed: "As long as the earth exists, seed time and harvest time, cold and heat, summer and winter, and day and night shall not cease." (Genesis 8:22)

☐ Optional. Leader: **What is the spiritual significance of the seasons in the context of Tu BeShvat?** Participants respond.

There is another symbolic meaning for the different wine colors. The *Zohar*[80] says: "Wine has two colors, white and red, which represent Mercy and Judgment ... White is from the Right Side [*Hesed*: Mercy, Love], red from the Left Side [*Gevurah*: Severity]." The four cups symbolize a pious person's evolving awareness of God's compassion within the world. We begin with white, which represents situations where it is easiest to recognize God's mercy, then slowly progress through pale and dark pink to red, when we finally recognize His mercy even in severity, even in suffering and affliction. Judgment (*Din*) is when we are unaware of God's goodness. We "sweeten [ameliorate] the judgments" when we realize that the ultimate source of all Severity (*Gevurah*) is Compassion (*Rahamim*) and that it is a vessel for Love (*Hesed*). When we see God's love and compassion even in suffering, we are in the Garden of Eden.

☐ Optional. Leader: **What else might the different colors of wine symbolize?** Participants respond.

THE FIRST CUP: WHITE WINE

☐ A participant recites:

The Holy One, blessed be He, said: "Just as wine can be a cause of trouble in this world, in the future I shall make it only a source of joy, as it says: 'And it shall come to pass on that day that the mountains shall drip with sweet wine' (Joel 3:18)." (*Vayikra Rabba* 12:5)

☐ All recite:

Wine symbolizes the secret of Oneness. It symbolizes the joy of the Divine Presence.

יַיִן הוּא רָז שֶׁל אֶחָד, רָז שֶׁל שִׂמְחַת הַשְּׁכִינָה.

☐ Leader: **Drink the first cup of wine meditatively, while uttering a silent prayer: "God, let me know the oneness of all reality and feel the joy of Your presence."**

☐ Lift the cup of white wine. All recite:

Blessed art Thou, O Lord our God, King of the Universe; Creator of the fruit of the vine.

בָּרוּךְ אַתָּה יְיָ, אֱלֹהֵינוּ מֶלֶךְ הָעוֹלָם, בּוֹרֵא פְּרִי הַגָּפֶן.

☐ Drink the wine. Then all recite:

**The mountains will drip with sweet wine,
and the hills will flow with it. (Amos 9:13)**

וְהִטִּיפוּ הֶהָרִים עָסִיס וְכָל הַגְּבָעוֹת תִּתְמוֹגַגְנָה.

SONG THEN MEDITATION

☐ Leader:

**Close your eyes and repeat the previous meditation on being
surrounded by and infused with the Divine Presence; go more
deeply into meditation. Pause Focus on the world of Action (*Asiyah*),
represented by fruits with shells. All movements in the world,
including your own actions, only happen by God's will. Resolve:
May all my deeds be for the sake of heaven.** (If the group has not
conversed for the Seder's first part, then, after concluding the
meditation:) **We can talk now.**

FRUITS WITH SHELLS: Pomegranates, nuts – such as walnuts,

almonds, pecans, pistachios, Brazil nuts,
coconuts– oranges, grapefruits, mangos, avocados, [these require
the blessing *ha-adamah*:] pineapples, watermelons, cantelopes,
honeydew melons, bananas, peanuts

Fruit for Thought from the Torah and the Rabbis

The Torah and particularly the Rabbis often saw hints of heavenly
meanings in the characteristics of fruit trees and fruits. This section
contains a selection of their teachings. May they inspire us to our own
thoughts of divine metaphors and meanings. On Rosh HaShanah it is
traditional to eat specific foods with symbolic meanings; on the New Year
of the Trees, all the fruits have symbolic meanings, if we can discern
them.[81] (A few comments that are not from the Torah or Rabbis have
been included in "Fruit for Thought" sections.)

☐ Here and in later "Fruit for Thought" sections, one or more participants each recites one teaching. Either recite teachings about all the fruits in a category, then eat those fruits together; or, proceed fruit by fruit– recite one or more teachings about pomegranates; then eat pomegranates.

POMEGRANATE

"The pomegranates have budded"– These are the little children who study Torah and sit in rows in their class like the seeds of a pomegranate. (*Shir HaShirim Rabba* 6:11)

Resh Lakish said: "Even the emptiest Jews are as full of mitzvot and good deeds as a pomegranate is of seeds." (*Yalkut Shimoni*, Shir HaShirim 4:3)

The Rabbis ask in the Talmud: How did Rabbi Meir continue to study with his teacher Elisha ben Abuya after the latter became a heretic? They said: "Rabbi Meir found a pomegranate. He ate its meat and threw away its peel." (*Hagiga* 15b)

Rabbi Schick of Breslov-New York writes: "When you eat a pomegranate [on Tu BeShvat], intend to justify every Jew, no matter who he is."[82] "By finding good points even in sinners and those far from God one can judge them favorably ... because they are as full of mitzvot as a pomegranate. This is the meaning of 'he ate its meat'– one values their good points, and as a result, 'he threw away its peel'– their bad side is nullifed. For when you find the good in Jewish souls, the bad is nullified."[83]

NUT

The People of Israel are like a walnut tree whose roots must remain uncovered for it to prosper. The roots hint at the holy Jewish Patriarchs and Matriarchs. If a Jew "covers his roots"– if he fails to keep before his eyes his holy roots– he will not prosper spiritually, for he will only do whatever he desires and commit unworthy deeds. Not so the person who always keeps his holy roots exposed before his eyes. He will be ashamed to sin when he considers his roots; so he will prosper [spiritually] and not sin. (*Midrash Talpiyot*, Ilanot[84])

The nutshell protects the fruit. ... And as long as the shell stays attached to the fruit, it too is protected. But as soon as it separates from the fruit, the shell is thrown into the garbage. So too with the

Jewish people: As long as they cling to the Sages, following their guidance [and protecting them], they [are protected and] inherit both this world and the next– but the moment they separate from them, they lose both worlds. (*Yalkut Shimoni*, Shir HaShirim 992)

Rabbi Berehya said: "Just as a walnut has four 'storerooms' around a central 'courtyard,' so in the desert, Israel had four flags, four camps, and the Tent of Meeting [the *Shechinah* (Divine Presence)] in the center." (*Shir HaShirim Rabba* 6:11)

Rabbi Tarfon compared the People of Israel to a pile of walnuts. If one walnut is removed, each and every nut in the pile is shaken and disturbed. So is it with Israel: When a single Jew is in distress, every other Jew is shaken by the trouble. (*Shir HaShirim Rabba* 6:11)

Why is Israel compared to a nut? Rabbi Azarya said: If a nut falls into the dirt, it can be wiped clean, washed, and restored to its edible condition. So too with Israel: No matter how much they are defiled by wrongdoing and sin during the year, when Yom Kippur comes, it makes atonement for them. (*Shir HaShirim Rabba* 6:11)

On Rosh HaShanah, we eat foods with symbolic meanings and the custom is not to eat nuts, for "nut" (*egoz*) is numerically equivalent to "sin" (*hait*)– 17[85]. Why then do we eat nuts on the New Year of the Trees? Because (*egoz*) is also the numerical equivalent of "good" (*tov*). Reverence and awe of God predominate on Rosh HaShanah, so we emphasize fear of sin. But on Tu BeShvat, love of God predominates; so we repent from love and resolve to do good.[86]

The Jewish people, who were sanctified at Mount Sinai, are compared to a nut. When the shell is broken, the nut emerges. When Israel were sanctified [and their evil inclination broken], they became soft and gentle [to God and to people[87]]. (*Yalkut Shimoni*, Shir HaShirim 992)

Just as a stone breaks open a nut, so the Torah, which is like a stone– as it says: "I will give you the tablets of stone" (Exodus 24:12)– can break open the hard shell around a person's heart. (*Shir HaShirim Rabba* 6:11[88])

Some nuts are easily cracked, opening almost by themselves; others are middling nuts; others are tough and hard-to-crack. So too with Israel: Some of them give *tzedaka* [charity] by themselves, some give when asked, but others are tough nuts, who do not give even when asked. (*Shir HaShirim Rabba* 6:11) We should each ask ourselves: Which kind of nut am I?

Rabbi Eliezer Shlomo Schick of Breslov-New York writes:
"The nut is a fruit that hints at the *Shechinah* (*Zohar*, Exodus 15).
It is surrounded by a hard shell. In order to merit to see and
experience God's glorious Divine Presence, blessed be He, a person
must break the hard shell that surrounds his mind. A person is
unable to experience and see His glorious Divine Presence, blessed
be He, because the way the Holy One, blessed be He, created the
world, His Light is covered by a hard shell [that surrounds the
world]. One must break the nutshell to get to the fruit. ... One must
also break the shell that surrounds every Jew, to find the hidden
good concealed within him. Every Jew has good concealed within,
but the shell– which represents his sins– hides and covers it.
Therefore, in even the worst person, who transgressed (God save us)
the whole Torah, one can find good points, which is the Godliness
within him, for the good is Godliness. But it is surrounded by a shell
due to his bad and deplorable deeds. ... Although a Jew may be
surrounded by a hard shell, what is within him is not contemptible.
If one will only break through the shell, one will find the good and
will be able to return him to God in repentance."[89]

ORANGE

Rabbi Yekutiel Yehudah of Tzanz-Klausenberg once reflected on
former generations when he was sitting at his festive table on Tu
BeShvat. He said: "Our holy ancestors and Rabbis were [not
desirous of worldly things and possessions; they were] satisfied with
little; their only hope and desire was to serve God and to study
Torah. I remember when I was a child ... that my holy mother and
teacher [Hayya Mindel] once brought an orange to the table and
gave every one of the children a section. One time, elsewhere, she
saw that people were each eating a whole orange at a meal and she
was upset. She said, "It's like gluttony!"[90]

Personal Reflections and Comments

☐ Leader: **Gaze at any of the fruits before you on the table. What
thoughts come to mind?** Participants comment.

On Tu BeShvat, I remember what my father and teacher, Mac
Buxbaum, of blessed memory, said when he wanted to impress on me
how poor the people were in Eastern Europe, where he came from. He

used to say that when he was a boy, "they would make a parade over a grapefruit." My father was telling me to be grateful for what I have, as the Rabbis say: "Who is rich? He who is happy with his portion [what God has given him]." (*Avot* 4:1)

☐ Eat fruits that have a thick, inedible rind or peel, and nuts.

THE SECOND CUP: PALE PINK WINE

☐ Drink the wine.

MEDITATION THEN SONG

☐ Leader:

Repeat the previous meditation and go deeper. Pause **As we sing, ascend to the world of Formation (*Yetzirah*), represented by fruits with pits. Arouse your feelings of love and awe for God: I long to be in God's presence!**

FRUITS WITH PITS: Dates, olives, apricots, peaches, plums, cherries, loquats, jujubes, hackberries

Fruit for Thought from the Torah and the Rabbis

OLIVE AND OLIVE OIL

The Jewish people is compared to the olive tree, which is unusual in having two flowers for each fruit. Jews also bring forth two "flowers"– doing mitzvot whether they are comfortable or afflicted. The two flowers also hint that when a Jew does a mitzvah, he desires to do it again; or, that when he does one mitzvah it will lead to his doing a second, as the Rabbis say: One mitzvah leads to another mitzvah. The two flowers of each olive also hint at the perfect unification of [the two aspects of God:] *Havaya* [Bringing Into Being] and *Adnut* [Lordship], which the mouth cannot utter nor the mind contemplate, because of the great perfection of their unification, more than coals are joined to fire and fire to coals. (*Midrash Talpiot*, Ilanot[91])

Rabbi Yohanan said: "Why is Israel compared to an olive? To teach you that just as an olive does not give its oil except when crushed, so too the Jewish people does not repent and return to God except after being crushed by suffering." (*Menachot* 53b) May we merit to repent in love and joy, out of expansiveness and with all good things.

Rabbi Yehoshuah ben Levi said: "Why is Israel compared to an olive tree? Because just as the leaves of the olive tree do not fall off either in summer or in winter, the Jewish people shall not be cast off, either in this world or in the World-to-Come." (*Menachot* 53b)

Rabbi Yirmiyah ben Eleazar said: "What is the meaning of the passage that says about the dove Noah sent out from the ark: 'Behold, a plucked olive leaf was in its mouth' (Genesis 8:11)? The dove said to the Holy One, blessed be He: 'Master of the World, may my sustenance be bitter as an olive but from Your hands, rather than being sweet as honey but from the hands of flesh and blood.'" (*Erubin* 18b)

Rabbi Menachem Mendel Schneersohn, the Lubavitcher Rebbe, taught on Tu BeShvat: "Olives are bitter. This implies that although a Jew's life must be characterized by sweetness and goodness, he must, in times of introspection, come to a state of bitterness when evaluating his spiritual achievements."[92] Perfect divine service is with joy. But at limited times of soul-accounting, a person must be bitter about his spiritual failures.

The Rabbis said: Olive oil teaches a lesson. If a drop of water falls into a cup of olive oil, an equal drop of oil spurts out of the cup. So too, if a drop of foolishness enters your heart, an equal amount of Torah wisdom exits; but if a drop of Torah enters your heart, an equal amount of foolishness exits. (*Shir HaShirim Rabba* 1:2)

The Rabbis taught: Just as olive oil [used for lamps] brings light to the world, so does the People of Israel bring light to the world, as it says: "Nations shall walk by your light" (Isaiah 60:3). (*Shir HaShirim Rabba* 1:2)

DATE

The prophetess Deborah, the wife of Lapidot, was judging Israel at that time. She used to sit under the date palm of Deborah between Ramah and Beit El in the hill country of Ephraim; and the

People of Israel came to her for judgment (Judges 4:4-5). Deborah dwelt in the city of Atarot and supported herself: She had date palms in Jericho, orchards in Ramah, olive trees that produced oil in Beit Sakia and Beit El, and grain and vegetable fields in Tur Malka (*Targum* on Judges 4:5).

Like the date palm tree, whose "heart" [from which the palm fronds grow[93]] points straight up toward the sky, the heart of Israel is directed to their Father in Heaven. (*Midrash Tehillim* 92:11)

Rabbi Hiyya bar Luliani said: "Why does the Psalm (92:13) say: 'The righteous shall flourish like a palm tree, and grow like a cedar in Lebanon'? Why are both trees mentioned? If the palm tree alone were mentioned, you might think that, like a palm tree, which when cut down does not produce new shoots from its stump, so too, when a righteous person stumbles, he will not rise again. Therefore, the cedar too is mentioned, for it grows new shoots from its stump. So too the righteous person perseveres and emerges renewed from his difficulties, as it says: 'A righteous man falls seven times but rises up again' (Proverbs 24:16). If the cedar alone were mentioned, you might think that although the righteous are tall like the cedar, like the cedar they give no fruit. That is why it says that they are also like the date palm, which gives fruit. What are the fruits of a righteous person? A legacy of Torah teachings, disciples, and faithful children." (*Ta'anit* 25a,b[94])

No part of the palm tree is wasted; every part may be used: Its dates are for eating, its lulav branches are for waving in praise on Sukkot, its dried up branches are thatch for roofing, its fibers are for ropes, its leaves for sieves, and its planed trunks for house beams. So is it with the Jewish people: Every one of our people is needed. Some are knowledgeable in *Tanach* [Bible], others in *Mishna*, others in *Agada* [talmudic legends]; still others do many mitzvot, and others do much charity. (*Bamidbar Rabba* 3:1)

PEACH

Once, in the time of the Second Temple, when Israel was suffering from a drought, the people went to Honi, a great tzaddik, and asked him to pray for rain. Honi drew a circle on the ground, stepped within it, and prayed: "Master of the World, Your children have turned to me because I am like a member of Your household. I swear to You that I won't leave this circle until You have compassion on Your children and bring them rain." The rains immediately began to fall. Rabbi Shimon ben Shetach said of Honi: "He is like a child who demands from his father, 'Give me walnuts, almonds, peaches, pomegranates!' and his father gives him whatever he wants." (*Ta'anit* 23a) Honi, who was like a child of his Heavenly Father, prayed for God to have compassion on His children. The Hasidic Rebbes teach that not only the great tzaddikim, but all of us can make demands of God, because He is our Father and will give us everything good if we ask Him.

Beware of admiring the peach too much, lest you find that you are unable to enjoy it. It is good to admire a tzaddik, but excessive admiration, which places him on a pedestal that is too high, negates the real benefit of his example: of being inspired to emulate his holy deeds.

Optional Practice: Overcoming Our Faults and Failures: An Imagery Exercise

A Jerusalem kabbalist, Colette Aboulker-Muscat, specializes in the use of imagery in spiritual practice. The following guided imagery exercise is based on her teaching.

☐ Leader (slowly and paced): Close your eyes and imagine that a beautiful peach tree is before you. There is a ladder leaning against the tree. Go up the ladder. There are peaches on the tree. Take one. Look at it in your hand and see that it grows in size. Then it opens. Notice inside any dark spots. These are your faults and failings– anger, pride, whatever they are. Pluck them out with your other hand and throw them away. The peach closes. It reduces to its usual size. You put it back on the tree. You descend the ladder. Open your eyes.

Personal Reflections and Comments

☐ Leader: **Gaze at any of the fruits before you on the table. What thoughts come to mind?** Participants comment.

"PROOF"

I sometimes humorously mention at a Tu BeShvat Seder that we can "prove" the close connection of the Jewish people to trees from their

Yiddish names!– Baum (Tree), my own name, Buxbaum (Box tree), Feigenbaum (Fig tree), Applebaum (Apple tree), Birnbaum (Pear tree), Nussbaum (Nut tree), Tanenbaum (Fir tree), Greenbaum (Green tree). I usually ask others at the table for additional "baum" names.

☐ Eat fruits that have a pit.

PEREK SHIRA (THE BOOK OF SONG)

The kabbalistic Book of Song, *Perek Shira*, says that all creatures, both animals and plants, sing songs praising their Creator. Rabbi Eliezer the Great said: "Everyone who studies this *Perek Shira* every day is promised that he is a son of the World-to-Come."[95] Rabbi Shalom of Belz always taught, on Tu BeShvat, his insights on *Perek Shira*.[96]

Rabbi Eliezer Shlomo Schick of Breslov-New York writes:

> You should know, my beloved children, that God, blessed be He, brings into being, enlivens, and keeps in existence all the Creation– inanimate, vegetable, animal, and human being. They are all the very essence of His divine life-energy, blessed be He. Everything is a garment for the light of the Infinite One, blessed be He. All created things are crying out and revealing awesome and wondrous revelations of His Godliness that hint to a person how to return to Him, blessed be He, as our Master [Rabbi Nachman of Bratzlav] said: "The glory of God cries out from all things, for 'the whole earth is full of His glory [the Divine Presence]' (Isaiah 6:3)." ... The whole creation is singing a song before Him, blessed be He, and this is the meaning of *Perek Shira*[97], the songs that all creatures– inanimate, vegetable, animal, human– sing before Him, blessed be He[a]. When a person merits to recite and to reflect on *Perek Shira*, he is promised that he will be a son of the World-to-Come. For someone who reflects well on inanimate, vegetable, animal, and human, and seeks, searches, and finds the Godliness that they reveal, and cleaves to the Infinite One, blessed be He, repents from love and all his sins are forgiven. ...[98]

---

a. See the Baal Shem Tov tale on p.26.

The following passages from *Perek Shira* specify which Torah verses the Garden of Eden and various fruit trees sing.

The Garden of Eden sings: "Awake, O north wind! And come, O south wind! Send a breeze over my garden, that the fragrance of its spices waft abroad. Let my Beloved enter His garden and eat its delicious fruits." (Song of Songs 4:16).

The fig tree sings: "He who guards the fig tree shall eat its fruit; so he who waits on his master shall be honored." (Proverbs 27:18)

The date tree sings: "The righteous shall flourish like the palm tree; he shall grow like a cedar in Lebanon." (Psalms 92:13)

The grapevine sings: "As the wine is found in the cluster, and they say, 'Do not destroy it, for a blessing is found in it': So will I do for My servants' sake, and not destroy them all." (Isaiah 65:8)

The pomegranate tree sings: "Your lips are like a scarlet ribbon and your mouth is lovely. Your cheeks are like halves of a pomegranate behind your veil." (Song of Songs 4:3)

The apple tree sings: "As an apple tree among the trees of the forest, so is my beloved among the young men. With delight I sat in his shade and his fruit was sweet to my taste." (Song of Songs 2:3).

THE DANCE OF TU BESHVAT *by A. Mordechai*

It was Tu BeShvat in the year 1943 during the Second World War, and I was among the Polish-Jewish refugees in the far reaches of the Soviet Union[99]. Tens of thousands of forlorn Jewish refugees, fleeing the Nazi invasion of the Soviet Union, gathered in Samarkand. Of all the war refugees there, the lot of the Jews was the worst. Because who would pity them? Who would extend to them a brotherly hand or favor them with a compassionate look? But, then, suddenly, there appeared a good angel in the form of Rabbi Rafael, of the Jewish community of Bukhara. He had all the virtues of a tzaddik, but above all, he was dedicated to emulating the hospitality of our father Abraham.

Rabbi Rafael's house, which his family had owned for many generations, had a very spacious courtyard. It was a miracle that the Communists had not expropriated this house from him. But even the "Red Commissars" treated the gentle and pure Rabbi Rafael respectfully. In any case, Jews who were uprooted, outcast, and homeless streamed through the gates into his large courtyard. And there, with Rabbi Rafael, they found a refuge and a sanctuary; they found help and support.

Rabbi Rafael always had a smiling face. Whenever a new visitor came– a sad and suffering refugee– he was greeted warmly. Rabbi Rafael's face glowed even more on Sabbaths and holidays, when he wore his colorful Bukharan robe. But anyone who had not seen the light shining from his face on Tu BeShvat had never seen holy joy in his life. Why did Rabbi Rafael rejoice so on Tu BeShvat? There were two reasons:

First of all, there were growing in Rabbi Rafael's courtyard a number of fruit trees. Since the winter in Samarkand leaves early, and Spring enters quickly, these fruit trees were already beginning to show the first signs of blossoms on Tu BeShvat. So it was possible to make blessings over them in honor of the New Year, the Rosh HaShanah, of the Trees, as these blessings appear in the ancient prayer books of the Bukharan Jews. Therefore, Rabbi Rafael's joy overflowed on Tu BeShvat.

Second, and perhaps this was the main reason, among Rabbi Rafael's fruit trees, was an apricot tree. Apricot trees grow also in the Holy Land, which was not true of the other trees that belonged to him. Therefore, the apricot tree was precious to him, because it reminded him of the Holy Land. So when Rabbi Rafael would see the apricot tree blossoming, his joy was boundless. The dream of his life, to see the Holy Land with his own eyes, sprouted anew right in front of him on that day.

When Rabbi Rafael felt his heart overflow with joy, he invited every refugee who had taken shelter with him, to be outside, in the shade of the fruit trees that were waking up from their frozen winter slumber; he gathered all his guests into his courtyard in honor of the Holiday of the Trees. Rabbi Rafael's joy was limitless. But how could he draw into his happiness and his overflowing joy all those crushed and broken Jews, whose whole world had been destroyed? He found a way. He took out from a hidden spot a bag of raisins and almonds. What? Raisins and almonds in the midst of this war and famine! Rabbi Rafael walked about his courtyard and, his eyes gleaming with affection– gave a generous handful of raisins and almonds to every refugee. That did the miracle. Those who were sorrowful and dejected revived all at once when they felt between their fingers the good-smelling and tasty raisins and almonds! It was like a gust of wind with good news from a world that once was and now had been destroyed. So they revived for a brief moment.

Rabbi Rafael always made the *shehecheyanu* blessing over an apricot from his tree. "Blessed art Thou ... who hast kept us in life, and sustained us, and enabled us to reach this season!"– he called out in his booming voice. Rabbi Rafael made blessings, with great devotion, on the fruits that he had managed to store up in complete secrecy, to keep for the joyous day of Tu BeShvat. Then, he melted in joy and began to dance in stormy ecstasy. Rabbi Rafael sang and danced in the courtyard in honor of the holiday. His eyes were raised to heaven and his heart was directed far away, eastward to our Holy Land. As he chewed the apricot, he inwardly intended to one day see our Holy Land and enjoy its fruits. Rabbi Rafael was dancing in Samarkand, but his heart was in Jerusalem.

The homeless and hapless Jewish refugees made the blessing of *shehecheyanu*. Then they joined in with Rabbi Rafael's singing, and danced with him in a circle, until their legs were swept away in the current of the dance. That is how Samarkand danced in honor of Tu BeShvat.[100]

THE THIRD CUP: REDDISH-PINK WINE

Lessons from Trees

The Torah prohibits wanton destruction of trees during wartime, and the verse asks rhetorically: "Is a tree of the field a man, to be besieged by you?" (Deuteronomy 20:19). The Rabbis frequently refer to this Torah verse in connection with Tu BeShvat, understanding it not as a question but as a statement, as if it meant: A man is like a tree of the field. They used this verse to draw many comparisons between people and trees and to teach many lessons.

☐ Optional. Leader: **The Rabbis say: A person is like a tree of the field. How are human beings like trees?** Participants comment.

Two of the Rabbis' main themes in connection with the verse: "A man is like a tree of the field," are the sanctity of the Creation and the environment, and hope in difficult times.

TO TEND THE GARDEN

☐ A participant recites:

The Torah says: "And the Lord God took the man and put him into the Garden of Eden to till it and to tend it." (Genesis 2:15)

The *Midrash* teaches: "The Holy One, blessed be He, led Adam through the Garden of Eden and said, 'I created all My beautiful and glorious works for your sake. Take heed not to corrupt or destroy My world, for if you corrupt it, there is no one to make it right after you.'" (*Kohelet Rabba* 7:13)

"When warring against a city that you must besiege a long time to capture, you must not destroy its [fruit] trees, wielding the ax against them. You may eat of them, but you must not cut them down. Is a tree of the field a man that you should besiege it?" (Deuteronomy 20:19-20)

The Rabbis said: "When someone cuts down a fruit tree, its cry goes from one end of the world to the other, but its voice is not heard." (*Pirke d'Rabbi Eliezer* 34:19)

The Rabbis derived from the teaching in Deuteronomy, the principle of *bal tashchit*– not to unnecessarily destroy any creature or creation.

The Baal Shem Tov provided mystic insight into the meaning of *bal tashchit.* He taught that everything in the world has in it a spark of the *Shechinah*, the Divine Presence, which gives that thing existence and vitality. Therefore, he said that a person should treat every creature and creation, even inanimate objects, with reverence; he should not unnecessarily break or damage anything, because it is Godliness.[101] A person with mystic awareness walks softly and talks softly. His very touch becomes soft, for he realizes that all around him, above him, and below him, there is nothing but God. If we must show reverence even to inanimate objects, how much more so to plants!

Four Anecdotes About Reverence for Plants

We can illustrate this teaching of reverence for trees and plants by four anecdotes.

Once, when Rabbi Nachman of Bratzlav was traveling with some disciples and they stopped at an inn, he slept outside, because of the nice weather. In the middle of the night he woke up screaming. When his disciples ran to him, he told them that the inn had been rebuilt with young trees that had not been allowed to reach maturity. And when you cut down a young tree, a sapling, before its time, it is as if you killed a person.[102]

I [Yitzhak Buxbaum] remember years ago, when I was in a spiritual mood while walking along the Mystic River in the Boston area, I saw two teenage boys fully bending over a sapling. I felt the pain of the tree, which I palpably realized was a living being.

Rabbi Yosef Yitzchok, the sixth Lubavitcher Rebbe, was once walking with his father, Rabbi Sholom Ber, the fifth Rebbe, and they were discussing the subject of divine providence. Rabbi Yosef Yitzchok, who was totally immersed in the conversation, plucked a leaf from a tree, shredded it, and scattered it in the wind. His father said to him, "How can you be so indifferent to a creature of God? The Holy One, blessed be He, created this leaf for some purpose; it has a body and divine vitality. How is its 'I' less than your 'I'?"[103]

Once, when Rabbi Arye Levin was walking in a field with Rabbi Avraham Yitzhak Kook (the first Chief Rabbi of Israel), and they were discussing Torah, he plucked a blade of grass or a flower. Rabbi Kook visibly trembled upon seeing this and said to him, "Believe me when I tell you that in my whole life I've never unnecessarily plucked a blade of grass or a flower, because the Rabbis say: 'Each blade of grass below has an angel Above that says to it, "Grow!"' 'Every blade of grass utters a word, every stone whispers a secret, every creature sings a song!'"[104] "These words, spoken from a pure and holy heart, became deeply embedded in my heart," said Rabbi Levin, "and from then on I began to feel pity for every creation."[105]

☐ Optional. Leader: **Would anyone like to share a thought, teaching, or suggestion for a project about protecting the environment?**

HOPE IN DIFFICULT TIMES

The Rabbis often say that at this time of year the trees seem, to the eye, lifeless. But yet they revive and produce fruit. Thus, Tu BeShvat teaches us not to despair and to trust in God, for a person is like a tree of the field. Rabbi Yisrael of Chortkov said:

When a person is down in his fortune and has lost all hope, he should ponder a tree in winter. Its leaves have fallen, its moisture has dried up, it is almost a dead stump in the ground. Then, suddenly, it begins to revive and to draw moisture from the earth. Slowly, it blossoms, then brings forth fruits. A person should learn from this not to despair, but to take hope and have courage, for he too is like a tree. If God wills it, he can in one second be lifted up and elevated. But he must have faith in God– who can accomplish anything– and in God's providence.[106]

The Chortkover applied this lesson to a person's spiritual life as well as to his worldly fortunes. He said that just as a withered tree gathers moisture and revives, so should a person whose soul feels dry and withered, gather and store up Torah and mitzvot, and, with God's help, he will [spiritually] revive.[107]

The Chortkover Rebbe applied this lesson to the Jewish people too: The prophet Isaiah spoke in God's name, saying: "Like the days of a tree shall be the days of My people" (65:22). During winter, a tree withers and sheds its leaves, standing like a bare monument. Yet, when Spring comes, it revives, blooms, sends out new branches, and thrives, because during the icy winter months it collected the sap that it needed to grow. So too, the Jewish people need to encourage themselves and strengthen their faith, for even when our bones have withered in the Exile we can renew ourselves and receive new life.[108]

On one Tu BeShvat, Rabbi Shlomo Carlebach said:

> Today is Rosh HaShanah for all the trees. It's a secret Rosh HaShanah. You know, you look at a tree from the outside [at this time], nobody knows the tree's at the end. Just God and the tree know. You see, friends, we all have little New Years between us and God. Nobody knows I'm at the end. Nobody will ever know how broken I am. Just me and God. And at that moment, God can give me a New Year.[109]

☐ Lift the cup and all recite:

On Tu BeShvat we should learn to be strong and to hope for good, for a person is like a tree of the field.[110]

A tree endures many winters; it dries out and seems to have reached its end; yet it lives to thrive and produce fruit again.

The Jewish people has survived many harsh winters, and we have held on to our hope in the Lord. We trust in God's mercies, for He will not abandon us. As we produced glorious fruit in the past, we will do so in the future.

Each Jew must say: I am like a tree of the field. I can endure winter by looking forward to the Spring, when God will renew me with new life. I trust in God. I lift the cup of salvation, for God's salvation comes in the blink of an eye and there is hope for a man of peace. Though I walk through the valley of the shadow of death, I will fear no evil, for You are with me" (Psalm 23:4). "And there," says the Lord, "I will give her her vineyards and make the valley of trouble a door of hope" (Hosea 2:17). May the Holy One, blessed be He, renew the fruit trees and us for a good year. May the new year and its blessings begin![111]

בְּיוֹם ט״ו בִּשְׁבָט אֲנַחְנוּ צְרִיכִים לִלְמוֹד לְהִתְחַזֵּק וּלְקַוּוֹת לְטוֹב, כִּי הָאָדָם עֵץ הַשָּׂדֶה. הָאִילָן סוֹבֵל חֲרָפִים רַבִּים. הוּא מִתְיַיבֵּשׁ וְנִדְמֶה כְּאִלּוּ הִגִּיעַ אֶל קִצּוֹ, וְאַף עַל פִּי כֵן הוּא נִשְׁאָר בַּחַיִּים וּמְשַׂגְשֵׂג וְנוֹתֵן פֵּירוֹת.

עַם יִשְׂרָאֵל עֲדַיִן נִשְׁאָר חַי וְקַיָּם אַחֲרֵי חֲרָפִים רַבִּים וְקָשִׁים וּמַחֲזִיקִים בְּתִקְוָותֵינוּ בַּיְיָ. אֲנַחְנוּ בּוֹטְחִים בְּרַחֲמָיו שֶׁלֹּא יַעַזְבֵנוּ וְלֹא יִטְּשֵׁנוּ. כְּמוֹ שֶׁאֲנַחְנוּ נָתַנּוּ פֵּירוֹת מְהוּלָלִים בֶּעָבָר כֵּן נִתֵּן פֵּירוֹת בֶּעָתִיד. כָּל יְהוּדִי חַיָּב לוֹמַר: אֲנִי כְּעֵץ הַשָּׂדֶה. יְכוֹלַנִי לִסְבּוֹל הַחֹרֶף כִּי אֲנִי מְצַפֶּה לִתְקוּפַת הָאָבִיב כְּשֶׁיְּיָ יְחַדֵּשׁ אוֹתִי וִיחַיֵּינִי. אֲנִי בּוֹטֵחַ בַּיְיָ. כּוֹס יְשׁוּעוֹת אֶשָּׂא, כִּי יְשׁוּעַת יְיָ כְּהֶרֶף עַיִן, וְיֵשׁ תִּקְוָה לְאִישׁ הַשָּׁלוֹם. גַּם כִּי אֵלֵךְ בְּגֵיא צַלְמָוֶת לֹא אִירָא רָע כִּי אַתָּה עִמָּדִי. וְנָתַתִּי לָהּ אֶת כְּרָמֶיהָ מִשָּׁם וְאֶת עֵמֶק עָכוֹר לְפֶתַח תִּקְוָה. יְהִי רָצוֹן שֶׁהַקָּדוֹשׁ בָּרוּךְ הוּא יְחַדֵּשׁ הָאִילָנוֹת וְאוֹתָנוּ לְשָׁנָה טוֹבָה וְתָחֵל הַשָּׁנָה הַחֲדָשָׁה וּבִרְכוֹתֶיהָ!

☐ Drink the wine.

SONG THEN MEDITATION

☐ Leader:

Repeat the meditation for being in God's presence and go deeper. Pause Ascend to the world of Creation (*Beriah*), represented by soft fruits. Think: Everything that exists is being recreated every moment. Let me know the Creator!

FRUITS THAT ARE TOTALLY EDIBLE: (these seeds are considered edible) Figs, grapes, raisins (which are dried grapes), carobs, apples, pears, blueberries, raspberries, quinces, kiwi fruits, persimmons (some persimmons have pits), [require the blessing *ha-adamah*:] strawberries

☐ A participant recites:

Praise the Lord!
Praise the Lord from the heavens,
Praise Him in the heights!
Praise Him all you angels,
Praise Him all His hosts!
Praise Him sun and moon,
Praise Him all you stars of light,
Praise Him you heaven of heavens,
And you waters that are above the heavens!
Let them praise the name of the Lord,
For He commanded and they were created.
He has established them for ever and ever;
He gave a decree which none shall transgress.
Praise the Lord from the earth,
You huge creatures of the sea,
And all that dwell in the depths,
Fire and hail, snow and fog,
Stormy winds, fulfilling His word!
Mountains and all hills,
Fruit trees and all cedars,
Wild beasts and all cattle,
Creeping things and winged birds,
Kings of the earth and all peoples,
Princes and all rulers of the earth,

Both young men and maidens,
Old men and children,
Let them praise the name of the Lord,
For His name alone is exalted;
His majesty is revealed in the earth and the heavens.
And He has lifted up His people's banner,
To the praise of all those who love Him,
To the Children of Israel,
The people near unto Him,
Praise the Lord!   (Psalm 148)

Fruit for Thought from the Torah and the Rabbis

THE VINE: GRAPE AND WINE

Moses sent twelve spies to the land of Canaan. "And they came
to the Valley of Eshkol and cut down from there a branch with a
single cluster of grapes, and they carried it on a pole between two
of them ..."   (Numbers 13:23)

Isaiah prophesies about the future of the Jewish people:
And they shall build houses and inhabit them;
And they shall plant vineyards and eat the fruit of them.
They shall not build and another inhabit;
They shall not plant and another eat;
For like the days of a tree shall be the days of My people,
And Mine elect shall long enjoy the work of their hands.
                                              (65:21,22)

The Sages taught: "Just as grapes provide both food and drink
[wine], so too the Jewish people has both Torah scholars and men
of deeds." (*Tanhuma* [Buber], parshat Lech Lecha 21)

Just as a vine has large and small clusters and the large ones hang
lower [because of their weight], so too, Israel: Whoever labors in
Torah and is greater in Torah, seems lower than his fellow [because
of his humility]. (*Vayikra Rabba* 36:2)

Just as a vine produces wine and vinegar, each requiring a
different blessing, so too must a Jew make a blessing over good and
over bad– over good: "Blessed is He who is good and does good;"
over bad: "Blessed is the just Judge." (*Vayikra Rabba* 36:2)

[Israel is God's vineyard.] Just as the guard of a vineyard watches from above [in a raised booth], so too does Israel's guardian watch from Above, as it says: "Behold, the guardian of Israel neither slumbers nor sleeps" (Psalms 121:4). (*Vayikra Rabba* 36:2)

FIG

Rabbi Yohanan said: "What is the meaning of: 'He who tends a fig tree will eat its fruit' (Proverbs 27:18)? Why is the Torah compared to a fig tree? Figs on a tree do not ripen all at once, but a little each day. Therefore, the longer one searches in the tree, the more figs one finds in it. So too with the Torah: The more one studies it, the more knowledge and wisdom one finds." (*Erubin* 54a)[112]

Why is the Torah compared to a fig? Because most fruits contain something inedible[113]: Dates have a pit, grapes have hard seeds, pomegranates have a peel. But every part of a fig is good to eat. So too with the Torah: Every part of it contains wisdom. (*Yalkut Shimoni*, Yehoshuah 2)[114]

Mari ben Mar said: "What is meant by the passage in Jeremiah (24:1): 'The Lord showed me this vision: Behold, there were two baskets of figs placed before the Temple of the Lord. One basket had very good figs, like first-ripe figs, but the other basket had very bad figs, so bad that they were inedible'? The good figs represent the truly righteous and the bad figs represent the grossly wicked.[115] Perhaps you might think that the latter have no hope and no chance of returning to God. But it says: 'The baskets'[116]– that is, both baskets– 'give forth their fragrance' (Song of Songs 7:14). Both these and those will in the future be fragrant." (*Erubin* 21a)

CAROB

Rabbi Yehudah said in the name of Rav: "Every day a heavenly voice goes out and says [about Hanina ben Dosa, a great tzaddik of the time of the Second Temple]: "The whole world is sustained because of My son Hanina, but My son Hanina is satisfied with a small portion of carobs from one Sabbath to the next." (*Berachot* 17b)

Rabbi Shimon bar Yohai, author of the *Zohar*, and his son Rabbi Eleazar fled from Roman persecution and hid in a cave. A miracle occurred: A carob tree and a fountain of water were created for them so that they would be able to survive for thirteen years until it was safe for them to leave their hiding place (*Shabbat* 33b). God cares for us even in the midst our troubles.

During times of persecution and starvation in ancient Israel, carobs that were fodder for goats became food for people. The Rabbis believed that being reduced to this poor food was a heavenly sign to repent. "Rabbi Aha said: 'It is written, "If you are willing and obedient, you shall eat the good of the land; but if you refuse and rebel, you shall be eaten by the sword [*herev*]" (Isaiah 1:19)– you shall eat carobs [*haruv*]. Rabbi Aha also said: 'The Jews need to eat carobs before they will repent.'" (*Vayikra Rabba* 13:4)

One day, Honi the Circle Drawer was journeying on the road and saw a man planting a carob tree. Honi asked him, "How long does it take for this tree to bear fruit?"

The man replied, "Seventy years."

Honi asked further, "Are you certain that you'll live another seventy years so that you'll eat its fruit?"

The man replied, "I found grown carob trees when I entered the world; as my ancestors planted them for me, so I too plant for my children and descendants." (*Ta'anit* 23a) We must provide for future generations, both materially and spiritually, just as the past generations provided for us.

APPLE

Rabbi Hamma ben Rabbi Hanina explained the verse: "As an apple tree among the trees of the forest, so is my beloved among the young men" (Song of Songs 2:3). Why are the People of Israel compared to an apple tree? Because just as the apples on a tree appear before its leaves [contrary to the normal order of the leaves preceding the fruit], so the Children of Israel [at Mount Sinai] said "We will do" before saying "We will hear" (*Shabbat* 88a).

The Rabbis say that when God heard the Israelites utter these words, He said: "Who taught this secret of the angels to My children?"[117] The angelic secret is to decide beforehand to do God's will, whatever it is; not to think, I'll consider what it is first and then I'll decide whether to do it or not. This secret allows you to overcome your evil inclination and your weakness; it is the level of an angel.

Rabbi Nehorai said: "When a daughter of Israel was crossing the Red Sea, and her baby on her arm began to cry, all she had to do was stretch out her hand and take an apple or a pomegranate from the midst of the sea and give it to him, as it says: 'He led them through the depths [of the sea] as through a desert' (Psalms 106:9). Just as they lacked nothing in the desert [of Sinai, when God supplied all their wants], so too they lacked nothing in the depths [of the Red Sea; all their wants were supplied]." (*Shmot Rabba* 21:10)

The *Zohar* says: "Just as apples have different colors, so the Holy One, blessed be He, appears in different aspects."[118] God appears in many aspects, according to the needs of His worshipers.

☐ Eat fruits that have no shell or pit and are totally edible.

THE FOURTH CUP: RED WINE

More Wine: "Who is Good and Does Good"

According to Jewish law, when one brings a better kind of wine to the table, one makes a special blessing, not: "who creates the fruit of the vine," but: "Blessed art Thou, O Lord our God, King of the Universe, who is good and does good" (*Baruch ata Adonay, Eloheinu melech haolam, hatov v'hamaitive*)[119]. It is fitting on Tu BeShvat to make this blessing over a fine Israeli red wine.

One makes a special blessing over wine, different from other drinks; and when a better wine is brought to the table, one shows added appreciation for God's goodness. Moreover, the "God is good and does good" (*hatov v'hamaitive*) blessing is said only when one drinks the better wine with a companion[120]: God bestows good and more good; He is good to me and good to others; there is overflowing good. Rabbi Baruch Shalom Ashlag once explained why his father, Rabbi Yehudah Leib Ashlag, only drank wine at a meal when he could make the blessing: "who is good and does good." "Because," he said, "this blessing is about the greatest matter of faith there is, for we must believe that the Creator is good and does good."[121]

The *hatov v'hamaitive* blessing over better wine also hints that we must imitate God in being good and doing good. When you truly realize that God is good and everything that happens to you is good, you are in the

Garden of Eden. When you yourself become good and do good, the Garden of Eden is in you. These are prime lessons for Tu BeShvat.

☐ Bring to the table a bottle of fine red wine. Fill the fourth cup to overflowing. Lift the cup, and all recite:

God is good with an overflowing goodness. Everything He does is for good. May I realize this in my own life and experience the Garden of Eden in this world. And I pray that, like my Creator, I may be good with an overflowing goodness to all people and to all living beings.

Blessed art Thou, O Lord our God, King of the Universe, who is good and does good.

יְיָ הוּא טוֹב וּמֵטִיב לְלֹא הַגְבָּלָה. כָּל מַה שֶׁהָרַחֲמָן עוֹשֶׂה לְטוֹב עוֹשֶׂה. יְהִי רָצוֹן שֶׁאֵדַע זֹאת בְּחַיַּי וְאֶרְאֶה גַּן עֵדֶן בָּעוֹלָם הַזֶּה. וַאֲנִי תְּפִלָּה שֶׁגַם אֲנִי בִּדְמוּתוֹ לְבוֹרְאִי אֶהְיֶה טוֹב וּמֵטִיב לְכָל הַבְּרִיּוֹת. בָּרוּךְ אַתָּה יְיָ, אֱלֹהֵינוּ מֶלֶךְ הָעוֹלָם, הַטּוֹב וְהַמֵּטִיב.

☐ Drink the wine.

FRAGRANT FRUITS: Apples, particularly the small plum-size lady apple (pomme d'api), quinces, some pears, fejoas, passion fruits, mangos, qumquats

The world of God's Nearness (*Atzilut*) can be suggested by a fruit's fragrant scent. According to the Rabbis, Godliness is fragrant. They often mention the "fragrance of the Garden of Eden." The *Zohar* teaches that the Tree of the Knowledge of Good and Evil represents the revealed Torah, the Torah's do's and don'ts, what is good and what is evil; the Tree of Life represents the Kabbalah, the concealed Torah, the inside of the Torah. Rabbi Shlomo Carlebach said that the Tree of Life is fragrant; the Tree of the Knowledge of Good and Evil is not. The spirituality of holy people who attain the inner truth of the Torah is charming and fragrant. Isaac said about Jacob: "See, the smell of my son is like the smell of a field which the Lord has blessed" (Genesis 27:27). The Rabbis said this was the fragrance of the Garden of Eden[122] and that it was the fragrance of a field of apple trees.[123] The *Zohar* says: "The apple tree has a finer fragrance than any other tree."[124] The Kabbalah often alludes to the Divine Presence (the *Shechinah*) in the Garden of Eden as the "Field of Holy Apple Trees."

☐ The Leader smells a fragrant fruit and recites a blessing. Participants answer "Amen," and fragrant fruits are passed around for everyone to smell.

Blessed art Thou, O Lord our God, King of the Universe, who gives a good fragrance to fruits.

בָּרוּךְ אַתָּה יְיָ, אֱלֹהֵינוּ מֶלֶךְ הָעוֹלָם, הַנּוֹתֵן רֵיחַ טוֹב בַּפֵּרוֹת.

MEDITATION

☐ Leader:

Inhale the fragrance of the fruit; then close your eyes and go deeper in meditation. Pause **Ascend to the world of Nearness (*Atzilut*). Don't move, don't feel, don't think. Transcend your body, feelings, and mind. Be still, and experience intimacy with ... the Soul of your soul.** After a time, the Leader ends the meditation.

MICAH'S FIG TREE

The prophet Micah speaks of the coming day when God's kingdom of Peace shall reign:

> They shall beat their swords into ploughshares
> And their spears into pruning hooks.
> Nation shall not lift up sword against nation,
> Neither shall they learn war any more.
> But they shall sit every man under his
> vine and under his fig tree,
> And none shall make them afraid,
> For the mouth of the Lord of Hosts has spoken.
> (4: 3,4)

There is a tale about Micah and his fig tree:

Micah was a Jew who lived on the outskirts of Jerusalem. He was a prophet, a visionary. He had a dream of a world of peace, where there was no hate or anger. He was a dreamer, but also a doer. He decided that if he could not make his dream come true in the larger world, he would at least make it come true in his own little world, of the people he encountered.

So he decided to build a house like the House on Mount Zion, in which there would be no hate or anger. He built his house without any wood, because he did not want to destroy any living trees. So he built it with stones. He did not want to carve the stones with metal tools, because metal is used to make weapons that destroy life. So he dug the foundation with his hands and built the house with uncut stones, like the altar in the Temple. He then planted a fig tree outside the house and, when it grew, he placed a table beneath its shade.

He wanted his house to be "a house of prayer for all peoples," like the Temple. So everybody could stay in Micah's house, to visit, and eat there; he gave them food as they sat under his tree. When guests left, birds flew down from the tree to eat the crumbs and were satisfied.

Micah never ate meat; he was a vegetarian. He did not want to take the life of any living creature. If he saw chickens or other birds being taken to market in cages on a wagon, he spent all his money to buy them and set them free. He would let them out of their cages and they would run and fly around Jerusalem.

Once, a prophet visited Micah (Micah did not know that this man was a prophet). After staying in Micah's house for a few days, he said he was about to leave and wanted to pay. He was testing Micah. Micah did not take money for his hospitality, but he did not want to seem self-important by making a fuss about refusing, so he quietly slipped the money back into the pocket of the prophet's robe. But a prophet, who can see from one end of the world to the other, can certainly see what is happening in his pocket. He said to Micah, "In heaven, they are so impressed by your vision of peace. I'm here to tell you that the day a child of yours eats a fig from the tree outside your house, the Messiah will come." At that time Micah was still childless.

Sadly, the next day, the Romans invaded Jerusalem. They destroyed the Temple and they destroyed Micah's house. But they could not destroy his dream. Micah went into exile with many other Jews.

Micah's fig tree produced fruit, and it yearned for one of Micah's children to eat its figs. So it vowed to follow the Jews into exile. They were exiled from country to country but the descendants of Micah's tree followed them. When the soil and climate permitted, trees grew and produced figs.

Hasidim serve figs to their children on Tu BeShvat because maybe, maybe, maybe one of the figs is a seed of a seed of a seed of Micah's fig tree. And maybe one of their children is a grandchild of a grandchild of Micah. And when one day, one of Micah's children eats a fig from his tree, the Messiah will come.[125]

THE DELIGHT IN CELEBRATING TU BESHVAT

The Soul's Delight

Why does the celebration of Tu BeShvat delight us? What is its mystery? Rabbi Menachem Mendel Schneersohn, the Lubavitcher Rebbe, answered this question.

The 15th of Shvat is not mentioned as a festival in the Written Torah (as, for example, Passover, Shavuot, and Sukkot are). Nor is it found in the Oral Law, as are Hanukkah and Purim, which are called *Yom Tov* [holidays] .... In the *Mishna*, the 15th of Shvat is mentioned as "Rosh HaShanah for Trees," but there is no mention of it being a festival. The idea of the 15th of Shvat being counted as a festival is a Jewish *custom*. Likewise, it is "a *custom* to increase in [eating] fruits" (Magen Avraham). ...

Something which is a "custom of Israel" (in our case the 15th of Shvat and eating fruit then) is so lofty that it can be expressed only as a "custom," and not in the Written Torah, and not even as a halacha to Moshe from Sinai [of the Oral Torah]. ... This explains the special aspect of a custom. The fulfillment of something mentioned specifically in the Written or Oral Torah does not provide especial delight for the Godly soul, for a Jew *must* fulfill all the mitzvot of the Torah. A "custom of Israel," on the other hand, and especially a custom that has been inaugurated only recently, provides delight for the Godly soul when it is performed, since it is not obligatory for a person (as, say, a halacha in the Oral Law is).

In other words: The reason for performing a "custom" (even before it has spread to and been accepted by all Jewry) is that it is an increase in Torah study and fulfillment of mitzvot in a manner even greater than that demanded by halacha. Thus, its fulfillment gives special delight to the person's Creator, as stated: "It gives Me pleasure that I have spoken and My will was done." The knowledge that a person has merited to cause God to have delight, automatically produces the greatest delight in the person.[126]

Thus, the Rebbe has answered our question: Why the celebration of Tu BeShvat delights us and what its mystery is.

God and Beauty

Another thought explains why Tu BeShvat delights us: The Kabbalah teaches that Beauty (*Tiferet*) is one of God's attributes, and He has filled His world with beauty to delight our eyes and other senses. Fruits (like flowers, butterflies, and birds) of lovely colors and graceful shapes are appreciated not only for their utilitarian value but also for their beauty. Thus, we make a special blessing when seeing beautiful trees and other creatures that God has created to delight human beings (see p.76). Part of the joy of Tu BeShvat comes from the beauty of the fruits themselves, which hint to us of Divine Beauty.

AFTER-BLESSING

Because of their importance, a special blessing is made after eating of the seven species for which the Land of Israel is praised– wheat, barley, grapes, figs, pomegranates, olives, and dates– or after drinking wine.[127]

☐ All recite:

Blessed art Thou, O Lord our God, King of the Universe, [after eating a grain dish (*mezonot*): for the sustenance and for the nourishment,] for the vine and the fruit of the vine, for the tree and the fruit of the tree, for the produce of the field, and for the desirable, good, and ample land, which Thou wast pleased to give as

an inheritance to our ancestors, that they might eat of its fruit and be satisfied with its goodness. Have mercy, O Lord our God, on Israel, Thy People, on Jerusalem, Thy City, on Zion, the dwelling-place of Thy Glory, and upon Thine altar and Thy Temple. Rebuild Jerusalem, the Holy City, speedily in our days, lead us up to it and make us rejoice in its rebuilding. There we will eat of its fruits and be satisfied with its goodness, and we will bless Thee for it, in holiness and purity. For Thou, O Lord, art good and doest good to all, and we will give Thee thanks for the Land, [for the sustenance,] for the fruit of the vine [for Israeli wine: the fruit of its vine], and for the fruits [for fruit of the five species from Israel: and for the Land and its fruits]. Blessed art Thou, O Lord, for the Land, [the sustenance and nourishment,] the fruit of the vine [or: the Land and its vine], and for the fruits [or: its fruits].

ברכה אחרונה מעין שלוש :

בָּרוּךְ אַתָּה יְיָ, אֱלֹהֵינוּ מֶלֶךְ הָעוֹלָם :

עַל מזונות - עַל הַמִּחְיָה וְעַל הַכַּלְכָּלָה :

עַל הַיַּיִן - עַל הַגֶּפֶן וְעַל פְּרִי הַגָּפֶן :

עַל פירות משבעת המינים - עַל הָעֵץ וְעַל פְּרִי הָעֵץ :

עַל מזונות וְיַיִן וְעַל פירות משבעת המינים בְּיַחד - עַל הַמִּחְיָה וְעַל הַכַּלְכָּלָה וְעַל הַגֶּפֶן וְעַל פְּרִי הַגֶּפֶן וְעַל הָעֵץ וְעַל פְּרִי הָעֵץ :

וְעַל תְּנוּבַת הַשָּׂדֶה וְעַל אֶרֶץ חֶמְדָּה טוֹבָה וּרְחָבָה שֶׁרָצִיתָ וְהִנְחַלְתָּ לַאֲבוֹתֵינוּ לֶאֱכֹל מִפִּרְיָהּ וְלִשְׂבּוֹעַ מִטּוּבָהּ, רַחֵם נָא יְיָ אֱלֹהֵינוּ עַל יִשְׂרָאֵל עַמֶּךָ וְעַל יְרוּשָׁלַיִם עִירֶךָ וְעַל צִיּוֹן מִשְׁכַּן כְּבוֹדֶךָ וְעַל מִזְבְּחֶךָ וְעַל הֵיכָלֶךָ, וּבְנֵה יְרוּשָׁלַיִם עִיר הַקֹּדֶשׁ בִּמְהֵרָה בְיָמֵינוּ וְהַעֲלֵנוּ לְתוֹכָהּ וְשַׂמְּחֵנוּ בְּבִנְיָנָהּ וְנֹאכַל מִפִּרְיָהּ וְנִשְׂבַּע מִטּוּבָהּ וּנְבָרֶכְךָ עָלֶיהָ בִּקְדֻשָּׁה וּבְטָהֳרָה :

כִּי אַתָּה יְיָ טוֹב וּמֵטִיב לַכֹּל וְנוֹדֶה לְּךָ עַל הָאָרֶץ [וְעַל הַמִּחְיָה] וְעַל פְּרִי הַגֶּפֶן [פְּרִי גַפְנָהּ] : וְעַל הַפֵּרוֹת [פֵּרוֹתֶיהָ]. בָּרוּךְ אַתָּה יְיָ עַל הָאָרֶץ [וְעַל הַמִּחְיָה וְעַל הַכַּלְכָּלָה] עַל פְּרִי הַגֶּפֶן [וְעַל פְּרִי גַפְנָהּ] וְעַל הַפֵּרוֹת [פֵּרוֹתֶיהָ].

CONCLUSION OF THE SEDER

☐ All recite:

Tu BeShvat anticipates the Final Redemption, the return to Israel and the return to the Garden of Eden.

"Behold, the days are coming," says the Lord,
"When the ploughman shall overtake the reaper
And the treader of grapes him who sows the seed;
The mountains shall drip with sweet wine,
And the hills shall flow with it.
I will restore the fortunes of My people Israel,
And they shall rebuild the ruined cities and inhabit them;
They shall plant vineyards and drink their wine,
And they shall make gardens and eat their fruit.
I will plant them upon their land
And they shall never again be plucked up out of the land
Which I have given them," says the Lord your God.
(Amos 9:13-15)

But you, O mountains of Israel,
Shall shoot forth your branches,
And yield your fruit to My people Israel,
For they will soon come home.
For, behold, I am for you, and I will turn to you,
And you shall be tilled and sown;
And I will multiply people upon you,
The whole house of Israel, all of it;
The cities shall be inhabited and the waste places rebuilt;
And I will multiply upon you man and beast;
And they shall increase and be fruitful;
And I will cause you to be inhabited
As in your former times,
And will do more good for you than ever before.
Then you will know that I am the Lord.
(Ezekiel 36:8-11)

Ezekiel continues:
Thus says the Lord God: "On the day that I cleanse you from all
your iniquities,

I will cause the cities to be inhabited
And the waste places shall be rebuilt.
The land that was desolate shall be tilled,
Instead of being the desolation that it was in the sight of all who
    passed by.
And they will say: "This land that was desolate
Has become like the Garden of Eden;
And the waste and the desolate and ruined cities are now inhabited
    and fortified."
Then the nations that are left round about you shall know that I,
    the Lord, have rebuilt the ruined places, and replanted that
    which was desolate;
I, the Lord, have spoken, and I will do it.

(vv.33-36)

God showed Ezekiel a vision in which a river issued from below the
heavenly Temple of the future. In those days, says the prophet:

All kinds of trees for food will grow up on both banks of the river.
Their leaves will not wither, nor their fruit fail; they will yield new
fruit every month, because the water that sustains them flows from
the Temple. Their fruits will serve as food, and their leaves for
healing. (47:12)

The Jewish people should learn from the tree, for it grows in two
directions at once: Its trunk, branches, and leaves continually strive
upward, while its roots dig deeper and deeper. So a Jew must reach
up to God, clinging to the Holy One, blessed be He, by Torah study
and prayer. At the same time, he must dig into the work of this
world: clinging to the *Shechinah* by serving fellow Jews and fellow
human beings, and by fulfilling the task of Adam and Eve of tending
God's Garden of Nature. We must care for the world around us: its
animals– from the mighty elephants and whales to the tiniest insects–
and its plants– from the mighty oaks and sequoias to the humblest
shrubs and grasses.[128]

The way to the Garden of Eden is the Torah.
    It is a Tree of Life to them that hold fast to it
And all that uphold it are happy.
Its ways are ways of pleasantness,
And all its paths are Peace. (Proverbs 3:18)

    Rabbi Oshiya said:

When King Solomon built the [first] Temple, he planted within it all kinds of fruit trees of gold that bore fruits in season. When the wind blew, the ripe fruits fell down, as it says: "it [the wind] shall shake, like Lebanon¹, its fruits" (Psalms 72:16). But when the enemies entered the Temple, the fruit trees withered, as it says: "the flower of Lebanon is mourning" (Nahum 1:4). In the future, the Holy One, blessed be He, shall restore these golden fruits of the Temple, as it says: "It shall blossom abundantly and rejoice, even with joy and singing; the glory of the Lebanon shall be given to it" (Isaiah 35:2). (*Yoma* 21b)

Rabbi Hiyya bar Ashi said in the name of Rav:
"In the future, all the barren trees in the Land of Israel will yield fruit, as it says: 'The trees have borne their fruit; fig tree and vine have yielded their strength' (Joel 2:22).'" (*Ketubot* 112b) ["the trees"– meaning *all* the trees, even those once barren and fruitless]

Rabbi Abba said:
"There is no more obvious sign of the End than this: 'You, O mountains of Israel, shall shoot forth your branches and yield your fruit to My people Israel, for they will soon be coming' (Ezekiel 36:8)." Rashi comments: "When the Land of Israel gives its fruits abundantly and generously, the End will be near; and there is no clearer sign of the End than this."[129]

Rabbi Menachem Mendel Schneersohn, the Lubavitcher Rebbe, said that when each Jew produces abundant "fruit," drawing many other Jews to God, that will be the sign of the coming of the Messiah.

May we go forth from this Tu BeShvat Seder renewed, purified, and healed, with a new heart and new eyes, to see the wonders of God's Nature, with its trees of all kinds and shapes, and its fruit of all kinds, shapes, and colors. And may we know, understand, and realize: that the glorious Presence of the Holy One, blessed be He, fills the earth, that *this* is the Garden of Eden, and we are its caretakers, that all human beings are made in God's image, and that

---

a. a name for the Temple

He has chosen the Land of Israel for His dwelling, and the People of
Israel as a banner to the nations. May it be so. Amen and amen.

The righteous shall flourish like a palm tree;
He shall grow like a cedar in Lebanon.
Planted in the House of the Lord,
They shall flourish in the courts of our God.
They shall still bring forth fruit in old age.
They shall be full of sap and richness;
To declare that the Lord is upright,
My Rock, in whom there is no unrighteousness.
(Psalm 92)

The Tu BeShvat Seder is now completed, according to its order and its
customs. As we have observed and fulfilled the Seder, so may we merit
to fulfill its inner meaning. May we enter Your Garden and rejoice in
Your Presence.

חֲסַל סִדּוּר ט"וּ בִּשְׁבָט כְּהִלְכָתוֹ וְחֻקָּתוֹ. כַּאֲשֶׁר זָכִינוּ לְסַדֵּר אוֹתוֹ כֵּן
נִזְכֶּה לְהַגְשִׁים כַּוָּנָתוֹ הַפְּנִימִית. יְהִי רָצוֹן שֶׁנִּכָּנֵס אֶל גַּנֶּךָ וְנִשְׂמַח
בִּשְׁכִינָתֶךָ.

The Rabbis teach:
In the future the Holy One, blessed be He, will make a circle dance
for the tzaddikim in the Garden of Eden. He will sit among them
and each will point with his finger to God in the center, as it says: "It
will be said on that day: 'This is our God, this is the One for whom
we waited that He would save us. This is the Lord for whom we
waited, and we will be glad and rejoice in His salvation'
(Isaiah 25:9)."[130]

[Hemdat Yamim describes the end of the Tu BeShvat Seder: "Then the
pious jump up from the tables and begin to dance."]

After the Tu BeShvat Seder, we look forward to the coming season
when the trees will blossom. The Kitzur Shulhan Aruh (Code of Jewish
Law) says: "On seeing [for the first time] fruit trees in blossom in the
Spring, one should say: 'Blessed art Thou, O Lord our God, King of the
Universe, whose world lacks nothing, and who created goodly creatures
and trees to benefit and delight human beings."[131] The Kitzur Shulhan
Aruh also says that on seeing goodly trees or beautiful animals, at any

time of year, we say: "Blessed art Thou, O Lord our God, King of the Universe, who has such as this in His world."[132]

When we have the eyes of the Six Days of Creation, of the Garden of Eden, we will see the goodness and beauty in the trees and in all creatures and creations, for God looked at everything He created and saw that it was good. When we see all the goodness and beauty that God has put in the natural world, we will also see His Goodness and His Beauty. As Tu BeShvat concludes, it is fitting to resolve to remember to say these blessings at the earliest opportunity.

ITEMS TO BUY AND PREPARE FOR A TU BESHVAT SEDER

1. Fruits: Most important are the five fruits of the "seven species": figs, dates, grapes, pomegranates (Chinese apples), and olives. Carobs, apples, walnuts, and almonds, are traditional. See the lists of fruits on pp.46,50,62.
2. Dried fruits: raisins, prunes, apricots, pears, etc.
3. Exotic fruits: Get at least a small amount so that everyone can have a taste. These fruits may be used for a *shehecheyanu* blessing.
4. Israeli fruits: Jaffa oranges or whatever else is available.
5. Nuts: See p.46. Get some nuts with shells (important), but most without shells.
6. Fragrant Fruits: See p.67.
7. Grains: This is optional. You can have challah or other bread. The traditional kabbalistic Tu BeShvat Seder includes a grain dish or cookies of wheat or barley. Beer can be used for barley.
8. Serve olives in olive oil or a dish that contains olive oil. Date or bee honey or honeycake.
9. Wine and grape juice: White and red wine. White and red grape juice, since some adults and children may not drink wine. You may want to purchase wines from Israel, especially a fine red wine for the *hatov v'hamaitive* blessing (see p.66).
10. Plates, utensils (although most items will be eaten by hand). A few knives, etc. to cut up fruits. A number of nutcrackers, and a hammer and screwdriver for breaking open coconuts. Bowls or trays for displaying and serving the items. Napkins. Cups for wine and grape juice.
11. Have a vessel available for collecting *tzedaka*.

Notes

1. *Sefer HaMo'adim*, vol.5, p.329, quoting *Hemdat Yamim*
2. This text is found in Sefarim Kedoshim: *Seder Hamisha Asar BeShvat v'Hamisha Asar BeAv.*
3. *Sefer HaMo'adim*, vol.5, p.357, "BeKahal Hasidim," by Yitzhak Arigur
4. The text has "new and old" fruits, alluding to Song of Songs 6:14. But since the *shehecheyanu* blessing is made over a "new" fruit not yet tasted that season, I have reversed the order for clarity.
5. *Rosh HaShanah LeIlanot*, p.28; bracketed comment about dipping olives in oil is clarified from p.60
6. *Rosh HaShanah LeIlanot*, Kuntres Tu BeShvat, p.26
7. *Sefer HaMo'adim*, vol.5, p.333
8. *Leket Tu BeShvat*, p.53, quoting *Sefer HaMo'adim*
9. *Orot Mordechai*, p.102
10. This recitation is largely taken from a duplicated Seder whose source I do not know.
11. This recitation is largely taken from a duplicated Seder of unknown authorship.
12. *parshat Terumah*, 168b
13. The literal meaning is "with righteousness" but the rabbis interpreted *tzedek* to mean *tzedaka*, charity. See *Baba Batra* 10a.
14. See *Baba Batra* 10a.
15. *Reshit Hochmah*, Sha'ar HaKedusha 4:21,23
16. See my *Jewish Spiritual Practices*, the chapters on "Meditation," pp.368-380 and "Eating and the Holy Meal," particularly pp.241-242, for many sources and quotes.
17. *Tehillah LeDavid*, p.144. *Ilana DeHayyei*, p.87, #79 quotes a teaching that the renewal of the trees on their New Year hints that a person should renew himself in old age.
18. *Hemdat Yamim* describes a Tu BeShvat Seder with four cups of wine-- white, white with a drop of red, half white and half red, and red with a drop of white (see p.8). But the Seder in *P'ri Aitz Hadar*, which was largely taken from *Hemdat Yamim*, mentions only two cups— white and red. I don't know the reason for this difference. I have combined the two traditions and use four cups of wine: white, pale pink, reddish pink, and red.
19. *Sanhedrin* 59b: "Rav said: 'Meat-eating was not permitted to Adam.'"
20. *Berachot* 32b referring to Proverbs 3:18
21. Rabbi Avraham Yehoshuah Heshel of Apt identifies the downward flow of divine life-energy in the Cosmic Tree of Life as "sap" (*Tehillah LeDavid*, p.147, quoting *Ohav Yisrael*).
22. Today [Tu BeShvat] is the New Year for fruits of the tree, when it comes to tithes. The new year begins from the 15th of Shvat, because most of the yearly rains have fallen, the sap begins to rise in the trees, and the fruits begin to develop. So too, on this date, there is a parallel Above; this is the New Year of the fruits of the Cosmic Tree, and there is a flow of divine energy to its fruits— the

worlds– through which it flows and descends down here below, to the fruits [of trees] and the angelic powers that rule over them. (*P'ri Aitz Hadar*, p.6)

23. *P'ri Aitz Hadar*, p.7, in Sefarim Kedoshim: *Seder Hamisha Asar BeShvat*
24. *Kiddushin* 6
25. I have combined different versions of this text.
26. *P'ri Aitz Hadar*, p.3, in Sefarim Kedoshim: *Seder Hamisha Asar BeShvat*
27. pp.3-4; the inserted bracketed remark is taken from p.7
28. *Bereshit Rabba* 26:6
29. *Rosh HaShanah LeIlanot*, p.12
30. *Tehillah LeDavid*, p.139, quoting *Marveh LeTzamai* (Israeli newspaper), edition 379-380, p.17
31. *Beit Yisrael*, Emet LeYaakov, p.76 (38b)
32. *Ilana DeHayyei*, p.62, #55, quoting *Ma'or v'Shemesh*.
33. Heard from Stephanie Bergash on Tu BeShvat in The Carlebach Shul, New York City, 1998.
34. The language of this declaration comes from two sources: The first part about the sign and memorial is from Rabbi Menahem Menashe in his book *Likkutei Menashe*, quoted in *S'de Ya'ar*, chapter 2, p.12, n.2; the second part about today being the New Year of the Trees, when the trees are judged is the language used by Rabbi Avraham Yaakov of Sadiger (*Beit Yisrael*, Emet LeYaakov, p.76 [38b]).
35. These words are derived from *Leket Tu BeShvat*, p.55, quoting *Leket Minhagei Paras*.
36. After his words that today is the trees' day of judgment (see n.34), Rabbi Avraham Yaakov of Sadiger continued: "And everything depends on the person" (his blessings and prayers), and he adduces Psalms 115:16 for proof; see also Psalms 8:7.
37. I derived this idea from a similar teaching of the S'fas Emes about the special blessing over bread (*Tehillah LeDavid*, p.140, quoting *S'fat Emet*).
38. *Berachot* 35a
39. *parshat Pinhas*, p.24
40. Based on a Tu BeShvat teaching of Rabbi Menachem Mendel Schneersohn, the Lubavitcher Rebbe (*Sichot in English*, vol.19, p.165)
41. *Rosh HaShanah LeIlanot*, p.47
42. *Reshimot Devarim*, vol.3, p.281, #12
43. *Sarei HaMaiya*, vol.3, p.168
44. *S'de Ya'ar*, Helek HaDrush, p.72, quoting *Darkei HaMusar*
45. *Kol Sippurei Baal Shem Tov*, vol.4, p.170
46. See my *Jewish Spiritual Practices*, p.411 for sources.
47. *S'de Ya'ar*, p.13
48. *Ketubot* 111b
49. *Ketubot* 112a; *Y.Shevi'it* 4
50. *Ketubot* 111a
51. *Y.Shevi'it* 3
52. Sefarim Kedoshim: *Seder Hamisha Asar BeShvat*, quoting *Minhagei Belz*
53. *S'de Ya'ar*, p.13

54. *P'ri Aitz Hadar* p.26 (in Sefarim Kedoshim: *Seder Hamisha Asar BeShvat*)
55. *S'de Ya'ar*, chapter 4, #5, p.49
56. *Rosh HaShanah LeIlanot*, p.24
57. See "Eating and the Holy Meal" in my *Jewish Spiritual Practices*, pp.225-279, for quotes and sources.
58. This order is based on Rabbi Solomon Ganzfried's *Code of Jewish Law* (*Kitzur Shulhan Aruh* 55:2).
59. This is based on the practice of Rabbi Avraham Yaakov of Sadiger on Tu BeShvat; see p.72.
60. *Kitzur Shulhan Aruh*, chapter 59
61. *Kitzur Shulhan Aruh* 59:14
62. On Sukkot, four plant species-- an etrog (citron), lulav (palm), willow and myrtle branches-- are ritually waved in the synagogue.
63. *Mishna Pe'ah* 1:1
64. *Shoshelet Spinka*, p.413
65. Siddur, daily Morning Service; *Mishna Pe'ah* 1:1
66. *Derech Tzaddikim* (Jerusalem: 1982), p.8.
67. *Shmot Rabba* 25:8
68. This phrase is derived from the words of Rabbi Yisrael of Rizhin (*S'de Ya'ar*, chapter 2, p.22, n.3, quoting *Tzemah Tzaddik*. The Rizhiner used to wear holiday clothes on Tu BeShvat, as if it were Rosh HaShanah.
69. Rabbi Avraham of Sokachtov said that after Tu BeShvat he felt a difference and a renewal in his *hiddushei* Torah, his ability to originate new Torah insights. (*Mivasair Tov: Mivhar Amarim Bain Adam LeHavero*, p.14.)
70. *Ohel Yissachar*, Imrei No'am, no pagination
71. Unfortunately, when I recorded this tale, I neglected to record its source, which is a hasidic book.
72. *Nitei Gavriel*, p.183, quoting *Birkat Eliyahu* (end)
73. *Berachot* 43b
74. This exercise was suggested by Sheryl Rosenberg of New York City.
75. This exercise is based on one suggested by Rabbi Everett Gendler in *The Jewish Holidays: A Guide and Commentary*, p.181.
76. See n.18.
77. See p.36.
78. *Berachot* 34b: "What is meant by: 'No eye has witnessed, O God, beside Thee!' (Isaiah 64:3)? Rabbi Yehoshuah ben Levi said: 'This refers to the wine stored in the grapes since the Six Days of Creation.'" *Yalkut Bereshit* 2: "When Rabbi Yehoshuah ben Levi visited Paradise, he was shown that each righteous person there has his own canopy from which issue four rivers of oil, milk, wine, and honey, and he is told: 'Eat your honey and drink your wine, for it has been waiting for you since the Six Days of Creation.'" Rabbi Eliezer Shlomo Schick of Breslov-New York writes: "One should intend, when drinking the wine [at the Tu BeShvat Feast], to draw down supernal lights and expanded states of consciousness ... [which are what the Rabbis call] the 'wine stored in the grapes since the

Six Days of Creation'"; see the full quote on p.25.

79. See the quote from *Hemdat Yamim* on p.8 in this booklet.

80. *parshat Pinhas*, p.24

81. *Nitei Gavriel*, p.202

82. *Rosh HaShanah LeIlanot*, p.56

83. *Rosh HaShanah LeIlanot*, p.58

84. *Tehillah LeDavid*, p.98

85. with the *kolel*

86. based on *Tehillah LeDavid*, pp.98-99

87. comment in the Lewin-Epstein edition of *Yalkut Shimoni* (Jerusalem, 1967)

88. This is slightly adapted, since the text is somewhat unclear, referring to the evil inclination as another stone (not nut) that the stone of the Torah breaks.

89. *Rosh HaShanah LeIlanot*, p.82

90. *Imrot Tzaddikim*, p.149, #2

91. *Tehillah LeDavid*, p.104

92. *Sichot in English*, vol.51, p.164

93. At the apex of the trunk, the part of the palm tree that produces the new fronds is shaped like a heart pointing to heaven.

94. as expounded in Rabbi Adin Steinsaltz's edition of the Talmud

95. *Rosh HaShanah LeIlanot*, Yeranenu Atzei HaYa'ar, p.6; no source listed

96. *Dover Shalom*, #230

97. Rabbi Schick calls the book *Pirkei Shira*.

98. *Rosh HaShanah LeIlanot*, Yeranenu Atzei HaYa'ar, Hakdama

99. The text has "Russia," which I've corrected.

100. Condensed from *Beit Yaakov* (Israeli monthly), edition 44/45, quoted in *Tehillah LeDavid*, p.225

101. *Keter Baal Shem Tov*, Kehot version, #218, p.56

102. *Hayyei Moharan*, Sichot Moharan, #88, p.62. In *Likkutei Moharan* 2:88, Rabbi Nachman quotes *Baba Batra* 26: "It is forbidden to cut down a tree before its time" (*Rosh HaShanah LeIlanot*, p.93).

103. *Kovetz Sippurim* 5731-5734, p.21, #4

104. This saying is in quotation marks; I don't know its source.

105. *Malachim Kevnei Adam*, p.239

106. Condensed from *Ginzei Yisrael*, quoted in Sefarim Kedoshim: *Seder Hamisha Asar BeShvat*

107. Condensed from *Ginzei Yisrael*, quoted in Sefarim Kedoshim: *Seder Hamisha Asar BeShvat*

108. Condensed from *Ginzei Yisrael*, quoted in Sefarim Kedoshim: *Seder Hamisha Asar BeShvat*

109. from a transcript of a tape made on Tu BeShvat, 1981 in Jerusalem

110. Rabbi Yisrael of Chortkov said: "Tu BeShvat comes to teach courage and hope to Israel." (*Tehillah LeDavid*, p.215)

111 the words of Rabbi Yaakov of Hosyatin (*Tehillah LeDavid*. p.84)

112. *S'de Ya'ar*, P'ri HaAitz, p.10

113. This rabbinic comment seems to differ from the kabbalistic Tu BeShvat Seder in which such seeds are considered edible.

114. Quoted in *S'de Ya'ar*, P'ri HaAitz, p.10

115. In the continuation, God explains to Jeremiah his prophetic vision. Note that Jeremiah sees a vision of fruit with symbolic meaning.

116. The word *duda* can mean both "mandrake" (love apple), as in the literal meaning of the verse in Song of Songs, or "basket."

117. *Shabbat* 88a

118. *parshat Aharei Mot*, p.74

119. See *Kitzur Shulḥan Aruḥ* 49:7-16 for laws about this blessing.

120. *Kitzur Shulḥan Aruḥ* 49:13

121. Rabbi Avraham Mordechai Gottlieb. *HaSulam: Pirkei Hayyeihem u'Mishnatam shel Rabboteinu HaKedoshim, HaAdmorim L'Veit Ashlag v'Talmideihem* (Jerusalem: 1997), p.32

122. *Midrash HaGadol*

123. *Ta'anit* 29b

124. *parshat Aharei Mot*, p.74

125. I heard this tale from Rabbi Sam Intrator on Tu BeShvat at The Carlebach Shul, New York City, 1998. The written source is *Sefer HaMo'adim*, vol.5, p.404-- a story called *Galut HaTamarim* ("The Exile of the Fig Trees") by Yehudah Steinberg. I have used both sources and retold the tale.

126. *Sichot in English*, vol.12, pp.189-192

127. *Kitzur Shulḥan Aruḥ* 51:7,8

128. This paragraph is adapted from a duplicated Seder with no name attached. I will happily credit the author in the future if I learn his identity.

129. *Leket Tu BeShvat*, p.2. No source is given for these quote. The first is in *Megillah* 17b, but Rabbi Abba is not mentioned.

130. *Ta'anit* 31, which reports this tradition: Rabbi Chelbo said in the name of Ulla, who quoted Rabbi Eleazar.

131. 60:1

132. 60:15

GLOSSARY

BEIT MIDRASH – Torah study hall

HALACHA – Jewish law

HEMDAT YAMIM – (*Choicest of Days*) Kabbalah book about the holidays

KIDDUSH – Blessing over the wine before a Sabbath or holiday meal

MIDRASH – Ancient rabbinic scriptural interpretation, often including parables, sayings, and stories

MISHNA – The ancient rabbinic text that is the core of the Talmud

ORLAH – The prohibition not to eat fruits for the first three years of a tree's life

P'RI AITZ HADAR – (*Fruit from a Fine Tree*) Kabbalistic Tu BeShvat Seder printed in *Hemdat Yamim* and also separately

SHEHECHEYANU – "Who kept us alive" blessing said on special occasions

SHECHINAH – Divine Presence

TZADDIK – (pl. *tzaddikim*) A holy man; Hasidic rebbe

ZOHAR – (*Splendor*) The main book of the Kabbalah

BIBLIOGRAPHY

Hebrew

Greenfeld, Arye Leibush. *Ilana DeHayyei: LeHamisha Asar BeShvat.* Monsey, New York: Ohel Torah, 1998.

Kurzweil, Aharon. *Leket Tu BeShvat BeHalacha U'v'Agada* (title page; cover says *Tu BeShvat– Rosh HaShanah LeIlanot*). Bnei Brak: Merkaz HaSefarim Bnei Brak, 1990.

Lewinsky, Yom-Tov. *Sefer HaMo'adim*, vol.5: Yemei Mo'ed v'Zikaron. Tel Aviv: D'vir, 1961.

Mandelbaum, David Avraham. *Tehillah LeDavid: Tu BeShvat BeHalacha U'v'Agada.* Jerusalem: Mosdot Imrei David, 1993.

Raz, Akiva Arye. *S'de Ya'ar: Tu BeShvat.* Jerusalem, 1993.

Schick, Eliezer Shlomo. *Rosh HaShanah LeIlanot.* Jerusalem: Hasidei Breslov.

Zinner, Gavriel. *Nitei Gavriel: Dinei u'Minhagei Purim* [includes a section on Tu BeShvat]. Brooklyn: Mazal, 1986.

Compiler not named. *Sefarim Kedoshim: Seder Hamisha Asar BeShvat v'Hamisha Asar BeAv.* Brooklyn: Beit Hillel, 1990. This book includes the text of *P'ri Aitz Hadar*, the traditional kabbalistic Tu BeShvat Seder.

English

Buxbaum, Yitzhak. A Person is Like A Tree: A Sourcebook for Tu BeShvat. 1999.

Buxbaum, Yitzhak. Jewish Spiritual Practices. Northvale, N.J: Jason Aronson, 1990.

Eckstein, Barry. Tu Bi'shevat Manual for Home-School-Community. New York: Jewish National Fund, 1989.

Fisher, Adam. Seder Tu Bishevat: The Festival of Trees. New York: CCAR Press, 1989.

Glatzer, Shoshana. A Tu Bi'shevat Seder. New York: Board of Jewish Education of Greater New York.

Strassfeld, Michael. The Jewish Holidays: A Guide and Commentary. Philadelphia: Harper & Row, 1985.

Waskow, Arthur. Seasons of Our Joy: A Handbook of Jewish Festivals. New York: Bantam, 1990.

IF YOU ENJOYED THIS BOOKLET AND BENEFITTED FROM IT

☐ **Why not send gift copies to friends or arrange for your synagogue or group to buy a set for your next Tu BeShvat Seder?**

A Tu BeShvat Seder can be purchased for $9.95 + $2.50 (S & H) = $12.45. For each additional copy, add: $9.95 + $0.50 (S & H) = $10.45. Ten copies cost $60 + $5 (S & H) = $65. Twenty copies and above, $5 per copy plus shipping costs at 15% of the order (10% of orders over $200). See the order form on p.91.

☐ **You will certainly enjoy Yitzhak Buxbaum's book *A Person is Like A Tree*: A Sourcebook for Tu BeShvat.**

Beside the section from which this booklet is largely drawn, *A Person is Like a Tree* also contains many more teachings from the Torah and Rabbis about fruits, and a great number of wonderful Hasidic and kabbalistic teachings and tales. This exciting material will make your Tu BeShvat Seder as delicious as a Passover Seder. Inquire from Yitzhak Buxbaum about price (see p.94).

☐ **Perhaps you might enjoy Volume 1 or 2 in The Jewish Spirit Booklet Series:**

Real Davvening:
Jewish Prayer as a Spiritual Practice and a Form of meditation for Beginning and Experienced Davveners

Learn to *davven* (pray) so that it moves you spiritually.

Simple traditional meditation techniques can lift your praying immeasurably higher than before, until you actually taste and experience the nearness of God. That is what is called *Real Davvening*.

This booklet will open the gates before you to one of the most important Jewish spiritual practices: *prayer*. It contains practical, easy-to-do teachings that will enliven your *davvening* and your Judaism.

Price: $7.95. Ten copies cost $60 + $5 (S & H) = $65

An Open Heart:
The Mystic Path of Loving People

The mystic teachings about loving your neighbor as yourself, from the Torah, Talmud, Midrash, Kabbalah, Hasidic and Musar sources. Exciting material found no where else.

"An Open Heart is a *kiddush HaShem,* it puts Judaism in such a good light!" (Dr. Arthur Green)

Price: $9.95.

Shipping & handling costs for Volumes 1 and 2 are the same as for Volume 3 above.

☐ Perhaps you might enjoy one of Yitzhak Buxbaum's books:

Jewish Spiritual Practices

Softcover, 757 pages
List price: $40. Discount price:
$35 (+ $3 for S & H) = $38

Once in a while I read a book that not only makes a profound impression but radically alters my lifestyle. Such a book is *Jewish Spiritual Practices* ..." (*Jerusalem Post*).

"*Jewish Spiritual Practices* is a very, very important book, one which the contemporary Jewish world has been in need of for many years. It is ... the first attempt at a comprehensive guidebook in English to the spiritual dimension of [Jewish religious practices]" (*Wellsprings* [Lubavitch hasidic magazine]).

"*Jewish Spiritual Practices* by Yitzhak Buxbaum ... recently was presented to the Dalai Lama [in India] by an American rabbi who wanted to explain Jewish spirituality to the religious leader." (*Publisher's Weekly*).

The Life and Teachings of Hillel

Hardcover, 376 pages
List price: $40. Discount price:
$35 (+ $3 for S & H)= $38

"Buxbaum is a patient and generous religious teacher, writing about Hillel in Hillel's own spirit. This book is filled with learning and profundity, allowing its subject to speak directly to the reader's heart." (Dr. Arthur Green)

Storytelling and Spirituality in Judaism

Softcover, 255 pages
List price: $30. Discount price:
$25 (+ $3 for S & H)= $28

The first and only book about sacred storytelling in Judaism and about the hasidic theology of storytelling.

ORDER FORM

To order copies of *A Tu BeShvat Seder*, (or any other books or booklets,) send a check payable to Yitzhak Buxbaum, along with this form or a duplicate, to the address on p.94.

Please send the following:

Title	Quantity (incl. shipping, etc.)	Price
A Tu BeShvat Seder	_____	_____
An Open Heart	_____	_____
Real Davvening	_____	_____
Jewish Spiritual Practices	_____	_____
The Life and Teachings of Hillel	_____	_____
Storytelling and Spirituality in Judaism	_____	_____

*NEW YORK STATE RESIDENTS:
For shipments sent to a New York address, add the appropriate sales tax for your area. New York State law requires that tax be paid on the full cost of the order, including shipping.

Subtotal
Sales tax* _____
TOTAL _____

You are invited to join
The Jewish Spirit Booklet Club

See the statement about the goals of The Jewish Spirit Booklet Series on p.2. Club membership only involves receiving information about publication of new booklets. To join, check the box.

☐ Please enroll me in The Jewish Spirit Booklet Club, to be kept informed about forthcoming booklets.

(*Print clearly*)

Name

Address

City   State   Zip

Maggid

YITZHAK BUXBAUM

Teacher • Storyteller • Author

YITZHAK BUXBAUM is an inspired and inspiring teacher and storyteller, one of those reviving the honorable calling of the *Maggid* (preacher), who in times past travelled from community to community to awaken Jews to the beauty of their tradition.

Mr. Buxbaum teaches and tells stories with warmth and humor. He often sets the mood by leading singing. And he creates the exciting and enlivening atmosphere of a special event, in which everyone is involved.

Judaism is communicated in a way to reach the committed as well as the curious, those who are near, along with those who are now far– but just need someone to offer them a welcome at the door.

Mr. Buxbaum's approach is not denominational or sectarian and is for Jews of all backgrounds. His programs are appropriate for different age-groups: teens, college-age, adults and seniors.

The programs are entertaining. They are also genuine spiritual experiences. As the Rabbis say: What comes from the heart, enters the heart.

Programs include: LECTURES on topics of Jewish spirituality and mysticism and STORYTELLING of hasidic tales. Inquire about lecture topics.

Mr. Buxbaum leads WORKSHOPS ON DAVVENING that can energize your congregation or havurah. He is available for FULLER SHABBAT PROGRAMS and as a SCHOLAR-IN-RESIDENCE.

Recommendations for
Yitzhak Buxbaum's Teaching and Storytelling

Yitzhak Buxbaum, author of *Jewish Spiritual Practices, The Life and Teachings of Hillel, Storytelling and Spirituality in Judaism, Real Davvening, An Open Heart,* and *A Tu BeShvat Seder* has lectured and told stories at synagogues, JCC's, Y's, Hillels, and retreats, producing enthusiastic responses. He has taught at CAJE conferences, Havurah Movement Summer Institutes, the Elat Chayyim Jewish Retreat Center, the New York Open Center, the New Age Center, and the renowned New School for Social Research (New York, N.Y.).

He was honored by being asked to address an audience of rabbis at The New York Board of Rabbis on the topic "The Quest for Spirituality."

"Many thanks for your presentation and for sharing your wonderful insights and delightful teaching manner with all of us." (Rabbi Jeremiah Wohlberg, President, New York Board of Rabbis)

"Yitzhak Buxbaum is a storyteller in the tradition of the great Hasidic masters. He retells their stories with penetrating insight into their relevance for the great and small actions of our lives. People of all backgrounds are powerfully affected by Yitzhak's unique Jewish presence." (Dr. Herb Levine, Hillel advisor, Franklin and Marshall College, Pa.)

"Yitzhak Buxbaum is a gifted spinner of tales. The audience sits enraptured as he unfolds a tale with skill and warmth." (Rabbi William Berkowitz, former head of the Jewish National Fund and Rabbi of Congregation B'nai Jeshurun, New York, N.Y.)

For a brochure and information about programs, contact:

YITZHAK BUXBAUM, Editor
The Jewish Spirit Booklet Series

144-39 Sanford Ave., Apt.6D
Flushing, New York 11355
(718) 539-5978